ADVANCE PRAISE FOR *HATE*

"One of life's hardest tasks is to tell natural allies they are wrong. Nadine Strossen is clear in a time of confusion, consistent in an era of hypocrisy, and brave in an environment of intimidation. Her book is a fitting capstone in a career in defense of our civil liberties."

—**Mitchell Daniels**, President,
Purdue University, and former Governor of Indiana

"Strossen has accomplished something remarkable in this slim book—she has ventured into a complex and heavily examined field and produced a book that is original, insightful, and clear-headed. My guess: this book will become the go-to work in the field."

—**Ronald Collins**, Harold S. Shefelman Scholar,
University of Washington School of Law, and
Publisher of *First Amendment News*

"Well-intentioned, but misguided, people today are clamoring for what amounts to censorship of speech they deem to be hateful. Nadine Strossen explains why the criminalization of advocacy, even advocacy of hateful ideas, imperils honorable freedoms. What's more, she provides a robust defense of a piece of old-fashioned, but oft-forgotten, wisdom: The safest—and most effective—way to fight bad ideas is not by limiting the right to free speech, but by exercising that right to counter them."

—**Robert P. George**, McCormick
Professor of Jurisprudence, Princeton University

HATE

INALIENABLE RIGHTS SERIES

. . .

GEOFFREY STONE AND OXFORD UNIVERSITY PRESS GRATEFULLY ACKNOWLEDGE THE INTEREST
AND SUPPORT OF THE FOLLOWING ORGANIZATIONS IN THE INALIENABLE RIGHTS SERIES: THE ALA;
THE CHICAGO HUMANITIES FESTIVAL; THE AMERICAN BAR ASSOCIATION; THE NATIONAL
CONSTITUTION CENTER; THE NATIONAL ARCHIVES

HATE

Why We Should Resist It with Free Speech, Not Censorship

Nadine Strossen

OXFORD
UNIVERSITY PRESS

OXFORD

UNIVERSITY PRESS

Oxford University Press is a department of the University of Oxford. It furthers
the University's objective of excellence in research, scholarship, and education
by publishing worldwide. Oxford is a registered trade mark of Oxford University
Press in the UK and certain other countries.

Published in the United States of America by Oxford University Press
198 Madison Avenue, New York, NY 10016, United States of America.

CIP data is on file at the Library of Congress
ISBN 978–0–19–085912–1

7 9 8 6

Printed by Sheridan Books, Inc., United States of America

This book is dedicated to Norman Dorsen and Aryeh Neier, key leaders of the ACLU during the Skokie controversy, inspiring human rights champions, and revered mentors.

"[T]he strongest weapon against hateful speech is not repression; it is more speech—the voices of tolerance that rally against bigotry . . . , and lift up . . . mutual respect."

—President Barack Obama

"In the end, we will remember not the words of our enemies, but the silence of our friends."

—Martin Luther King, Jr.

"[H]ardly any of the voices that should have been raised in moral protest against Nazism were to be heard in Germany or the territories conquered by the Reich. Where political and religious leaders did speak out against the Nazis, notably in . . . Denmark, most Jews were saved. Those Jews who died . . . were victims of the silence of Europe's moral leadership as they were victims of the Nazis."

—Aryeh Neier, ACLU executive director
during the Skokie litigation

Contents

. . .

Acknowledgments

...

This book benefited immeasurably from the enormous contributions by the superb Series Editor, Geoffrey Stone, who brought to bear his unsurpassed First Amendment expertise, brilliant analysis, and meticulous editing talent. The book is far better than it could have been without his extraordinary, generous attention at all levels, from the most nuanced wording choices to the most challenging overarching questions of doctrine, policy, and principle.

Others who generously read and helpfully commented on drafts were Floyd Abrams, Ron Collins, Bob Corn-Revere, Norman Finkelstein, Eli Noam, and Ben Wizner.

Special encouragement was provided by Carol Mann, an outstanding literary agent who was accurately described by a mutual friend as a gifted "midwife" in bringing books to life; Aryeh Neier; and Karen Gantz Zahler. Those who especially facilitated the book are New York Law School's Dean Anthony Crowell and Associate Dean Bill LaPiana, who granted me a sabbatical leave for Spring '17, with substantial Research Assistant support. I also thank Professors Martin Flaherty, Doni Gewirtzman, Frank Munger, and

Jerry Vildostegui for teaching the students who had been enrolled in my Spring '17 courses, as well as all those students who conveyed thoughtful messages that they would miss me in the classroom, but were looking forward to reading the book.

NYLS Librarians Michael McCarthy and Carolyn Hasselmann provided valuable research support, as did the following current and former NYLS students: Josephine Bahn, Jakub Brodowski, Michael Collins, Dennis Futoryan, Alexis Granell, Lisabeth Jorgensen, Nana Khachaturyan, Kasey Kimball, Dale Mackey, Michael McKeown, Stefano Perez, Julio Piccirillo, Rachel Searle, Richard Shea, Alexander Weinman, and Jacques Zelnik. Further appreciated research assistance was provided by Chris Jennison, and Faculty Assistant Stan Schwartz helped greatly on many fronts. Others at NYLS who provided special assistance include Assistant Dean Oral Hope, Claude Abner, Silvia Alvarez, Tuan Bui, Regina Chung, Dana Ninons, Aracelis Norberto, Elizabeth Thomas, Robert Torres, and Jeffrey Yu.

At Oxford University Press, I was fortunate to benefit from the expertise and dedication of Irene Barnard, Leslie Johnson, Dave McBride, Erin Meehan, Niko Pfund, Sarah Russo, Claire Sibley, Lucie Taylor, Paul Tompsett, Reneysh Vittal, Wendy Walker, Robin Wane, and Enid Zafran.

I am indebted to the scholars whose work has informed and inspired this book. For their influential pieces documenting adverse impacts of hateful speech and the importance of societal responses, including counterspeech, I am grateful to Richard Delgado, Stanley Fish, Charles Lawrence, Mari Matsuda, Jean Stefancic, Alexander Tsesis, and Jeremy Waldron. I am also grateful to those First Amendment activists and scholars with whom I have collaborated most closely, and whose work has provided the background "continuo" to this book, including Floyd Abrams, Yaman Akdeniz, Lee Bollinger, Agnès Callamard, Ron Collins, Bob Corn-Revere, Donald

Downs, David Goldberger, Joel Gora, Marjorie Heins, Jameel Jaffer, Peter Molnar, Burt Neuborne, Robert Post, Flemming Rose, Jeff Rosen, Robert Sedler, Steve Simpson, David Skover, Geoffrey Stone, Kathleen Sullivan, Trevor Timm, William Van Alstyne, Eugene Volokh, and James Weinstein, as well as many others who are active with the free speech organizations with which I have worked most closely: the ACLU (American Civil Liberties Union), FIRE (Foundation for Individual Rights in Education), and NCAC (National Coalition Against Censorship).

Others who made meaningful contributions are Nancy Abraham, David Burstein, Steve M. Cohen, Joseph Fornieri, Jonathan Haidt, Matthew Hoffman, Elizabeth K. Jackson, Peter Molnar, Dennis Parker, Becky Roiphe, Lee Rowland, Robert Schachter, Ruti Teitel, Raafat S. Toss, and Michelle Zierler.

I was fortunate to do much of the work on this book while being inspired by the beautiful live music performed at restaurants near my New Milford, Connecticut home by talented musicians, including Missy Alexander, John Bolger, Rob Brereton, Bob Brophy, Al Burgasser, Chuck Cundari, Chris Ellis, Eric Gatten, Nancy Janutolo, Mike Latini, Don Lowe, Suzy Marker, Doug Mathewson, Greg McClure, Felicia Michael, Jim Moker, Jim Nowak, Bill Petkanas, Phil Spillane, Guy Tino, Pat Walker, Nancy Walsh, and John Wood. For providing such congenial environments for writing, I'd also like to thank Joe Casimiro, Al and Johana Marchena, Luisa and Sergio Ragosta, and David and Senka Thompson. All of us raised our voices, along with many other neighbors, against hateful expression that in August 2017 temporarily defaced property in our community, but whose enduring effect has been to renew our commitment to overcome hatred and discrimination.

My final thanks go to the two most important men in my life: my father, Woodrow J. Strossen, who endured the horrors of the Buchenwald forced labor camp, resisted Nazi oppression, and forged a new life in a new country, ensuring that his daughter would never take life, liberty, or "equal justice under law" for granted; and my husband, Eli M. Noam, who has been the most perfect partner for enriching all aspects of my life, including the process of writing this book.

Editor's Note

. . .

We hold these truths to be self-evident, that all men are created equal, that they are endowed by their Creator with certain unalienable Rights. . . .

—*The Declaration of Independence*

It is difficult to think of anyone better suited to write about the idea of "hate speech" than Nadine Strossen, who served as president of the American Civil Liberties Union from 1991 to 2008. Strossen has dedicated her career to the defense of civil liberties and to the First Amendment. She is one of our nation's foremost champions of free speech. It is therefore more than fitting that at this turbulent time in our nation's history she should re-enter the debate in an effort to shed light on some of the issues that divide our nation today.

In *HATE: Why We Should Resist It with Free Speech, Not Censorship*, Strossen explores the natural and understandable reasons why thoughtful and well-meaning people want to silence "hate speech" and the compelling but often forgotten reasons why, in our free and democratic society, we must resist that temptation. Her point is not that "hate speech" is harmless, but that there are better ways to address it than censorship.

To make this case, Strossen explains the central meaning of our First Amendment and identifies the essential principles that frame our nation's commitment to the freedom of speech. But as fundamental as those principles are to our national values and traditions, she recognizes that there are some circumstances in which what people refer to as "hate speech" can, in fact, be restricted consistent with our Constitution. What she rejects, though, is the proposition that *"constitutionally protected* hate speech" should be censored because of its reviled viewpoint or its potentially harmful effects.

Strossen explores a broad range of important and complex issues, including the difficulty of drafting an anti–"hate speech" law that is both internally consistent and coherent, the failure of "hate speech" laws in other nations to solve the problems they are designed to address, the abuse of "hate speech" laws in other nations to manipulate the political process and to disadvantage the very minorities who are the intended beneficiaries of the legislation, and the many alternative methods that are available to address the harms potentially caused by "hate speech" without engaging in censorship.

In the end, Strossen concludes that "hate speech" laws do more harm than good, even though adopting them might be morally satisfying. Not only are they incompatible with core First Amendment principles, but they simply don't work and they are ultimately unnecessary. There are, in short, better ways to achieve the goals that such laws are said by their proponents to achieve.

In this work, Strossen stakes out a bold and important claim about how best to protect *both* equality and freedom. Anyone who wants to advocate for "hate speech" laws and policies in the future now has the "devil's advocate" right at hand. No one can address this issue in the foreseeable future without taking on this formidable and compelling analysis. It lays the foundation for all debates on this issue for years to come.

Geoffrey R. Stone
February 2018

Key Terms and Concepts

...

"The real issue in every free speech controversy is this: whether the state can punish all words which have some tendency, however remote, to bring about acts in violation of law, or only words which directly incite to acts in violation of law."
—Harvard Law School professor Zechariah Chafee

I did not include citations within this book; however, a list of my sources is available at www.nyls.edu/nadinestrossen.

In this book, I strive to discuss important, complex legal concepts clearly and concisely, but without oversimplifying. This task is especially challenging because the very term "hate speech," as well as other terms that recur in discussions about it, lack any specific, generally accepted definition. Given the inconsistent usages of key terms, debates on this topic have often been plagued by confusion. To minimize such confusion, I introduce below (in alphabetical order) the most important terms and definitions. These definitions also introduce a major argument against "hate speech" laws. They lay out the two cardinal free speech principles that all such laws inherently violate, especially endangering minority views and speakers: the emergency and viewpoint neutrality principles.

Some readers might prefer to skip this section now and instead refer to it as a complement to later chapters.

BAD TENDENCY (OR HARMFUL TENDENCY) AND EMERGENCY TESTS

These terms refer to two diametrically different tests that the U.S. Supreme Court has used, during different historical periods, for determining when government may suppress speech because it might cause harm. This is the key question concerning not only "hate speech," but also, as Chafee observed, all free speech issues.

Until the second half of the twentieth century, the Court held that government could constitutionally punish speech based on its feared "bad" or harmful "tendency": a vague, general fear that the speech might indirectly contribute to some possible harm, at some indefinite future time. (I prefer the term "harmful tendency" because it more clearly describes the speech's feared negative impact, but I will use the terms synonymously.) In practical effect, this test licensed the government to punish any speech whose ideas it disfavored, including speech that criticized government policies or officials.

In path-breaking dissenting opinions in the early twentieth century, Justices Oliver Wendell Holmes and Louis Brandeis rejected the bad tendency test, and instead laid out the stricter emergency test, which the Court finally unanimously adopted in the second half of the twentieth century. Under this test, the government may punish speech about public issues only when, in context, it poses an emergency: only when it directly, demonstrably, and imminently causes certain specific, objectively ascertainable serious harms that cannot be averted by non-censorial measures, the most important of which are counterspeech and law enforcement. In the past, the Court sometimes has used the phrase "clear and present danger" to describe this test, though it has invoked that phrase inconsistently. The term "emergency test" more clearly captures the strict criteria that the Court has rightly been enforcing for the past half-century.

BIAS CRIME OR HATE CRIME

These terms refer to criminal acts, such as assaults or vandalism, when the perpetrators deliberately select the victimized persons or property for discriminatory reasons. Because these crimes are believed to cause additional harm both to the victims and to society, they are subject to enhanced punishment.

CONSTITUTIONALLY PROTECTED "HATE SPEECH"

I use this phrase to underscore a key fact that is not well understood: that not all speech connoted by the vague phrase "hate speech" is constitutionally protected. Although the Supreme Court has never recognized a special category of "hate speech" that is excluded from First Amendment protection based on its message alone, government may restrict some speech with a hateful, discriminatory message (as well as speech that conveys other messages) if, in context, it directly causes specific imminent serious harm, thus satisfying the emergency test. Moreover, as I explain in Chapter 3, there are other contexts in which "hate speech" (as well as speech with other messages) may be restricted, in both the public and private sectors. Thus, the term "constitutionally protected hate speech" refers to "hate speech" that some people seek to censor but that the First Amendment protects.

COUNTERSPEECH

This term refers to any speech that counters or responds to speech with a message that the speaker rejects, including "hate speech." Counterspeech may address various audiences, including the speaker and others who share the speaker's views, the people the speech disparages, and the general public. In content, it may include denunciations or refutations of the message, support for the people the speech disparages, and information that seeks to alter the views of the speaker and others who might be sympathetic to those views. For any speech that has a feared harmful tendency but does not satisfy the emergency test, the Supreme Court has held that the constitutionally permissible response is counterspeech, not censorship.

DISFAVORED, DISTURBING, OR FEARED MESSAGES

I use these terms to summarize the three major potential negative impacts attributed to constitutionally protected "hate speech," which proponents of "hate speech" laws cite as justifying such laws, but which cannot justify the laws consistent with the fundamental emergency and viewpoint neutrality principles (on viewpoint neutrality, see below). Censoring views solely because they are "disfavored," no matter how deeply, directly violates the viewpoint neutrality rule. That rule is also violated when government suppresses speech about public issues, including "hate speech," because its views might have a "disturbing" impact on the emotions or psyches of some audience members. Since any such negative impact would flow from the speech's message, punishing speech on this rationale is tantamount to punishing its message. Finally, the emergency test bars punishing messages because of a fear that they might contribute to potential harmful conduct at some future time. In short, stating that government may not punish "hate speech" (or speech with other messages) solely because of its "disfavored, disturbing, or feared message" encapsulates the viewpoint neutrality and emergency principles.

"HATE SPEECH"

This term has no single legal definition, and in our popular discourse it has been used loosely to demonize a wide array of disfavored views. Its generally understood core meaning is speech that expresses hateful or discriminatory views about certain groups that historically have been subject to discrimination (such as African Americans, Jews, women, and LGBT persons) or about certain personal characteristics that have been the basis of discrimination (such as race, religion, gender, and sexual orientation). To underscore that the term has no single specific meaning, I, like some other commentators, put it in quotation marks.

"HATE SPEECH" LAW

I use this term to refer to any regulation of constitutionally protected "hate speech" by any government authority, including a public university. (Often such campus regulations are called "codes.") Such a law regulates "hate speech" even though it does not directly cause specific imminent serious harm, and it therefore violates both the viewpoint neutrality and emergency principles.

POLITICAL SPEECH

The Supreme Court often uses this term to refer to speech about public issues, which the Court consistently has held to be entitled to the strongest First Amendment protection, given its essential role in our democratic republic. As the Court declared in a 1964 case: "Speech concerning public affairs is more than self-expression; it is the essence of self-government." Notwithstanding the wide-ranging array of speech that has been castigated as "hate speech," by its very nature it expresses views on topics of public concern, ranging from race relations, to gender discrimination, to immigration policies. In a 2011 case that overturned the punishment that a state had imposed on vitriolic "hate speech" against Catholics, gay people, and military personnel, the Supreme Court declared that because the speech addressed "public issues," it "occupies the highest rung of the hierarchy of First Amendment values, and is entitled to special protection."

VIEWPOINT NEUTRALITY

This phrase refers to a principle that the Supreme Court has enforced, with increasing strictness, since the second half of the twentieth century, hailing it as "the bedrock" of our freedom of speech. Sometimes referred to as "content neutrality," this prin-ciple bars government from regulating speech solely because the speech's message, idea, or viewpoint is disfavored, or feared to be dangerous, by government officials or community members. As the Court has explained, any such "viewpoint-based" or "view-point-discriminatory" regulation would subvert not only individual liberty, but also our democratic self-government, because of the danger that officials would enforce it to "suppress unpopular ideas or information or manipulate public debate." In contrast, government may regulate speech when its message inflicts an independent harm, "such that there is no realistic possibility that official suppression of ideas is afoot." Crimes that consist of such expression include fraud, perjury, and bribery. Similarly, government may punish child pornography because it harms an actual minor in the production process.

Notwithstanding the viewpoint neutrality rule, the Supreme Court has held that a "few," "narrow" categories of speech, defined by their messages, should receive no First Amendment protection, or only reduced protection. (These rulings also constitute exceptions to the emergency test.) These unprotected or less protected categories of speech include obscenity, commercial advertising, and defamation; they never have included "hate speech." Over time, the Court has narrowed both the list of such categories and their definitions.

HATE

Introduction

As we face the challenge of countering ever-more-prevalent discriminatory and divisive attitudes and actions in our society, the word "hate" has been increasingly prominent in our political discourse. As experience teaches, anyone can be both accused of and subjected to "hatred" based on a wide range of personal characteristics and beliefs. The terms "hate speech" and "hate crimes" are used to demonize and to call for punishing a broad array of expression, including political discourse that is integral to our democracy.

The term "hate speech" is not a legal term of art, with a specific definition; rather, it is deployed to stigmatize and to suppress widely varying expression. The most generally understood meaning of "hate speech" is expression that conveys hateful or discriminatory views against specific individuals or groups, particularly those who have historically faced discrimination.

Beyond this core meaning, many people have hurled the epithet "hate speech" against a diverse range of messages that they reject, including messages about many important public policy issues. Moreover, too much rhetoric equates "hate speech" with violent criminal conduct. On many campuses, for example, students complain that they have been "assaulted" when they are exposed to ideas that offend them, or even if they learn that a provocative speaker has been invited to campus. This false equation between controversial ideas and physical violence fuels unwarranted calls for outlawing and punishing ideas, along with violence.

To be sure, campuses and other arenas in our society must strive to be inclusive, to make everyone welcome, especially those who traditionally have been excluded or marginalized. But that inclusivity must also extend to those who voice unpopular ideas, especially on campus, where ideas should be most freely aired, discussed, and debated. Encountering "unwelcome" ideas, including those that are hateful and discriminatory, is essential for honing our abilities to analyze, criticize, and refute them. On that point, I would like to invoke the inaugural convocation address by Ruth Simmons, Brown University's president from 2001 to 2012, the first African-American president of any Ivy League university, and Brown's first female president:

> You know something that I hate? When people say, "That doesn't make me feel good about myself." I say, "That's not what you're here for." . . . I believe that learning at its best is the antithesis of comfort. [I]f you come to this [campus] for comfort, I would urge you to walk [through] yon iron gate. . . . But if you seek betterment for yourself, for your community and posterity, stay and fight.

Discussions about "hate speech" have been clouded by conclusory condemnations, conflating many kinds of expression and action. Instead, we must draw critical distinctions between ideas that are disfavored, disturbing, or feared, which should be protected, and actions that are discriminatory or violent, which should be punished. My mission in this work is to refute the argument that the United States, following the lead of many other nations, should adopt a broad concept of illegal "hate speech," and to demonstrate why such a course would not only violate fundamental precepts of our democracy but also do more harm than good.

THE ESSENTIAL DISTINCTION BETWEEN PROTECTED AND PUNISHABLE "HATE SPEECH"

Debates about these issues are often marred by widespread confusion about the governing free speech principles. Too many people, including even some lawyers, wrongly assert that under our Constitution "hate speech" is either absolutely protected or completely unprotected. Neither statement is accurate.

On the one hand, many who argue that we should revise our law to empower government to punish "hate speech" wrongly assume that such speech is now *absolutely* protected. In support of their proposals, they cite many examples of speech that already is subject to sanction in the United States, consistent with longstanding free speech principles. For example, they regularly point to speech that constitutes a genuine threat or targeted harassment, and thus directly causes specific imminent serious harm, making it already punishable consistent with the emergency principle.

On the other hand, too many people wrongly assert that "hate speech is not free speech," assuming that speech with a hateful message is automatically excluded from First Amendment protection. Consistent with the cardinal viewpoint neutrality principle, however, government may not punish "hate speech" (or speech conveying *any* particular point of view) merely because some of us—even the vast majority of us—consider its views or ideas objectionable or even abhorrent. For that reason, no matter what adjective we might use to excoriate speech whose ideas we disfavor—including "hateful," "abusive," "unwelcome," "offensive," "dangerous," or "violent" (to cite some epithets that are invoked by advocates of suppressing the designated speech)—such disfavor alone does not warrant censoring the speech.

Moreover, speech may not be censored because its message might have a disturbing impact on the hearts or minds of some audience members. Viewpoint-based restrictions pose the greatest danger to the core value underlying the First Amendment: our right as individuals to make our own choices about what ideas we choose to express, receive, and believe. Because they distort public debate, viewpoint-based regulations are also antithetical to our democratic political system. Additionally, they violate equality principles because, reflecting majoritarian political pressures, they generally target unpopular, minority, and dissenting views and speakers. Censorship of "hate speech" is also unjustified by the speech's feared harmful tendency: the generalized fear that it might indirectly contribute to future negative conduct by some people who hear or read it.

These speech-protective precepts are not based on a presumption that speech cannot cause harm. To the contrary, we cherish speech precisely because of its unique capacity to influence us, both positively and negatively. But even though speech can contribute to potential harms, it would be more harmful to both individuals and society to empower the government to suppress speech for that reason, except consistent with the emergency and viewpoint neutrality principles. This book substantiates that conclusion with many examples from many different countries.

The Supreme Court strongly reaffirmed the foregoing First Amendment principles in a 2011 case in which it upheld the right of individuals to engage in extremely hurtful and offensive speech: picketing outside the funerals of military veterans with signs conveying hateful views about military personnel, Catholics, the pope, and gay men and lesbians. As the Court explained:

> Speech is powerful. It can stir people to action, move them to tears of both joy and sorrow, and—as it did here—inflict great pain. [W]e cannot react to that pain by punishing the speaker. As a Nation we have chosen a different course—to protect even hurtful speech on public issues to ensure that we do not stifle public debate.

The Court's near-unanimity in this case is noteworthy, and typical of its free speech rulings. In recent decades, the Court has been closely divided ideologically, often splitting 5–4 on other constitutional controversies. But justices across the ideological spectrum have consistently been united by strong support for the core freedom of speech principles, even when the speech conveys hateful and hated views.

This robust understanding of our First Amendment should likewise transcend partisan divides in our political sphere, because the underlying principles protect all speakers—and all audience members—whatever our views, and whoever we are. That critical point was stressed in the midst of the civil rights movement by a 1961 New York court ruling that upheld the free speech rights of an American Nazi to convey racist ideas, consistent with the viewpoint neutrality and emergency principles. The judge explained that these principles also redounded to the benefit of the civil rights activists who were conveying precisely the opposite, antiracist ideas, and who consistently were threatened with censorship in communities where *their* ideas were despised and feared, including the many campuses that excluded them:

> [T]he unpopularity of views, . . . their obnoxiousness . . . is not enough [to justify suppressing them]. Otherwise, the . . . antiracist . . . could be suppressed, if he undertakes to speak in "restricted" areas; and one who asks that public schools be open indiscriminately to all ethnic groups could be lawfully suppressed, if only he choose to speak where persuasion is needed most.

The fact that "hate speech" laws inevitably endanger views across the political spectrum is confirmed by recent experience under such laws in European countries. In a September 2017 essay, entitled "In Europe, Hate Speech Laws Are Often Used to Suppress and Punish Left-Wing Viewpoints," journalist Glenn Greenwald writes:

> Many Americans who long for Europe's hate speech restrictions assume that those laws are used to outlaw and punish expression of the bigoted ideas they most hate: racism, homophobia, Islamophobia, misogyny. Often, such laws are used that way. . . . But hate speech restrictions . . . in those countries . . . have frequently been used to constrain and sanction a wide range of political views that many left-wing censorship advocates would never dream could be deemed "hateful," and even against opinions which many of them likely share.

If we allowed government to suppress speech that might exert a negative influence on our minds or actions, then no speech would be safe. As Supreme Court Justice Oliver Wendell Holmes declared in a landmark 1919 dissent, in which he strongly repudiated the majority's bad tendency doctrine, "Every idea is an incitement." He did not mean by this statement that government may therefore suppress every idea, but rather the opposite: that government may suppress speech only when it directly causes specific, imminent, and serious harm.

As history teaches, permitting the government to punish speech based on any lesser connection between the speech and the feared harm would be a license for witch hunts—literally, as well as figuratively. Justice Louis Brandeis reminded us of this danger in his 1927 opinion in *Whitney v. California*, which Justice Holmes joined. After rejecting the majority's bad tendency standard, and its conclusion that the government could constitutionally punish Socialist Party activist Anita Whitney because her socialist advocacy might lead to "terrorism and violence," Brandeis wrote: "Fear of serious injury cannot alone justify suppression of free speech. . . . Men feared witches and burnt women." Accordingly, he articulated the highly speech-protective emergency standard that the Court finally unanimously endorsed in 1969: "Only an emergency can justify repression." Brandeis added that if the message's potential danger does not rise to the level of an emergency, the proper response is "more speech, not enforced silence."

The "hate speech" laws that many other countries now enforce, which license government to punish speech solely because its message is disfavored, disturbing, or feared, too often are enforced to suppress today's counterparts of Anita Whitney: those who express unpopular, dissenting views. It would hardly constitute progress for the United States to revert to a legal regime that enables officials to silence their critics.

MORE SPEECH, NOT LESS

Violent and discriminatory conduct must be swiftly punished, and speech conveying discriminatory, hateful ideas should be strongly rebutted. But punishing ideas we consider hateful or discriminatory not only violates the fundamental free speech principles outlined above; it also may well increase intergroup distrust and discrimination rather than reducing them. Evidence suggests that none of us is immune from "implicit" or unconscious biases that pervade our society, with its entrenched structural discrimination. Therefore, speech that reflects discriminatory stereotypes can often result from ignorance or insensitivity rather than malevolence. Of course, we must vigorously combat bias, including of the unintended variety. But the tools for doing so should be calibrated appropriately. Someone who negligently conveys stereotyped views is likely to respond more positively to constructive educational outreach than to accusations of and punishment for "hate speech." Indeed, as I discuss in Chapter 8, even for people who consciously harbor and express hateful views, educational strategies are more promising than censorship for altering such views and curbing their influence.

Just as "hate speech" and bias crimes are, alas, abounding, so too are resources for countering them, with a wealth of information, training, and organizations that empower all of us to speak up both for ourselves, if we are disparaged, and for others whom such speech targets. Also abounding are non-censorial measures for curbing the potential harm to which constitutionally protected "hate speech" is feared to contribute: discrimination, violence, and psychic injuries. The recently emergent interdisciplinary field of "hate studies" explores these kinds of non-censorial interventions, and human rights activists around the world have advocated increased reliance on them.

Especially positive is the increasing counterspeech we have been hearing from members of groups who have been disparaged by "hate speech," as well as from many other community members and leaders. This rising resistance to hateful words and deeds through the force of free speech—while also resisting the force of either censorship or violence—has been encouragingly evident in the face of demonstrations by "alt-right" and similar groups. We have witnessed a remarkable and bipartisan outpouring of speech and peaceful demonstrations that have denounced hateful ideologies and violence, and that have celebrated our nation's renewed commitments to equality, inclusivity, and intergroup harmony. This counterspeech chorus reaffirms the First Amendment's essential role in promoting these fundamental goals.

CHAPTER ONE

Overview

THIS CHAPTER PRESENTS a brief overview of the "hate speech" controversy. It provides background for the more in-depth analysis of subsequent chapters and a foundation for further reflection, discussion, and debate.

WHAT IS "HATE SPEECH"?

Myriad political controversies, and the heated rhetoric they often provoke, have generated charges and counter-charges of "hate speech." For example, members of the Black Lives Matter movement have been accused of "hate speech" against police officers, whereas many critiques of the Black Lives Matter movement have been denounced as "hate speech" against its supporters or against African Americans generally. Nathan Damigo, founder and leader of the white nationalist group "Identity Evropa," whose membership is restricted to people of "European, non-Semitic heritage," repudiates terms such as "racist" and "supremacist" as "anti-white hate speech."

Those who decry "white privilege" have been accused of "hate speech" against white people. Evangelical Christians who charge that LGBT sexuality is sinful have been accused of "hate speech" against gay men and lesbians, whereas those who make these charges against evangelical Christians have been accused of religious "hate speech." Similarly, critics of some Islamic teachings about women have accused some imams of "hate speech" against women, whereas these critics have in turn been accused of "Islamophobia," or "hate speech" against Muslims.

The epithet "hate speech" has also been used to stigmatize a wide array of controversial speech, including "fake" news, advocacy of terrorism, burning the American flag, "revenge porn," and anti-abortion demonstrations. Ultimately, what links all the variegated expression that has been attacked as "hate speech" is that the attackers disfavor—indeed, often hate—its messages, and for that reason seek to suppress them.

"HATE SPEECH" LAWS ENDANGER BOTH FREEDOM
AND EQUALITY

"Free speech is not only minorities' best friend . . . it's our only reliable friend."
—Jonathan Rauch, Senior Fellow, Brookings Institution,
and LGBT rights advocate

"[E]very great champion of African American freedom in our history—including Frederick Douglass, W.E.B. DuBois, and Martin Luther King, Jr.—has also been a warrior for freedom of expression."
—University of Pennsylvania professor Jonathan Zimmerman

Despite the varying definitions that have been adopted and proposed in "hate speech" laws, they all share two fundamental First Amendment flaws: they violate the cardinal viewpoint neutrality and emergency principles by permitting government to suppress speech solely because its message is disfavored, disturbing, or feared, and not because it directly causes imminent serious harm. Empowering government to choose the words and ideas we may not utter or listen to for these reasons stifles our freedom of thought, which is the essence of individual autonomy, and also an essential building block for democratic self-government.

Moreover, as I explain in greater detail in Chapter 4, "hate speech" laws also share a third basic First Amendment flaw, which flows from the first two: they are unduly vague and impermissibly overbroad, thus necessitating enforcement according to the subjective standards of complainants and enforcing authorities. While "hate speech" laws can be drafted with differing degrees of precision and breadth, they all center on concepts that call for subjective judgments, starting with the very concept of "hate" itself. Because these laws do not comply with the emergency or viewpoint neutrality principles, they lack the constraints that those principles impose on government discretion. Once government is authorized to suppress speech because of a feared harmful tendency or because of its disfavored, disturbing viewpoint, government has largely unfettered censorial power. In the United States, virtually all campus "hate speech" codes that courts have reviewed have been struck down on grounds of undue vagueness and overbreadth. Likewise, the language that has been used in other countries' "hate speech" laws demonstrates that, despite their many differences in detail, they all license government to make discretionary, subjective judgments targeting an expansive range of speech.

Given these fundamental First Amendment problems with "hate speech" laws, such laws end up stifling expression that even their proponents agree should be protected as part of the vibrant public discourse and dissent essential for our democratic self-government. This point was well stated by Eleanor Holmes Norton, an African-American civil rights lawyer who was the first woman to chair the Equal Employment Opportunity Commission, and who has been the longtime District of Columbia Representative in Congress. Referring to campus "hate speech" codes, she said: "It is technically impossible to write an anti-speech code that cannot be twisted against speech nobody means to bar. It has been tried and tried and tried."

Yes, "hate speech" may well have negative impacts. The old nursery rhyme is wrong when it declares that "Sticks and stones may break my bones, but words will never hurt me." Having been vilified with anti-Semitic and misogynist expression myself, I speak from experience. The reason why I still believe that we should continue to protect "hate speech" is well summarized by another old saying: "The cure is worse than the disease." Even worse than speech's potential power to harm individuals and society is government's potential power to do likewise, by enforcing "hate speech" laws. Predictably, this elastic power will be used to silence dissenting ideas, unpopular speakers, and disempowered groups. To avert this danger, the Supreme Court steadily has reduced government's power to punish speech solely because its message is disfavored, disturbing, or feared. Instead, government may punish speech that relates to public issues, including "hate speech," only when it directly causes a specific, imminent, serious harm, such as inciting imminent violent or illegal conduct. These requirements curb government's censorial power, reducing the risk that it will be wielded only or primarily to suppress unpopular ideas.

Unleashing government's power to silence ideas that are disfavored, disturbing, or feared not only undermines liberty and democracy; it also subverts the equality goals that animate "hate speech" laws. Such laws are predictably enforced to suppress unpopular speakers and ideas, and too often they even are enforced to stifle speech of the vulnerable, marginalized minority groups they are designed to protect.

These problems follow from the premises of "hate speech" law proponents themselves. They contend that our societal institutions, including the criminal and civil justice systems, reflect entrenched racism and other types of discrimination. They also point to the implicit or unconscious biases that our culture has engrained in us. Given these realities, it is predictable that the institutions and individuals enforcing "hate speech" laws will not do so in a way that is helpful to minorities. The actual enforcement record of "hate speech" laws around the world, discussed throughout this book, demonstrates that this predictable pattern in fact has materialized, including in developed democracies.

Recognizing this problem, some major proponents of "hate speech" laws in the United States have proposed that the laws should be enforced only when the speech is directed against groups that traditionally have been subject to discrimination. By favoring some speakers and messages over others, this approach squarely violates fundamental precepts of both free speech and equality. This approach is also bedeviled by practical complexities in application, as even its proponents acknowledge. Consider just one illustration of this problem. It comes from law professor Mari Matsuda's influential 1989 article, which argues that we should punish messages "of racial inferiority" that are "directed against a historically oppressed group" and are "persecutorial, hateful, and degrading." She acknowledges many problems in applying these criteria, including when the specified language "is used by one subordinated person to lash out at another."

Equal rights movements always have depended on robust freedom of speech, in particular the viewpoint neutrality and emergency principles, which shelter the egalitarian ideas that many have considered harmful, hateful, disturbing, and dangerous. By definition, ideas that challenge the status quo and advocate law reform tend to be seen in a negative light by the majority or the power elite. That certainly has been true of expression challenging racial injustice. The leading pro-slavery advocate, Senator John C. Calhoun, argued that abolitionists who criticized slavery "libeled the South and inflicted emotional injury." During the 1830s, many Southern states enacted laws suppressing abolitionist speech, which was feared to spur violence—in particular, slave rebellions—and indeed to threaten the nation's very survival. Legal historian Michael Kent Curtis has observed that even many Northerners shared the widespread "assumption that abolitionist publications would lead to slave rebellions." Likewise, Martin Luther King, Jr.'s historic letter came from a Birmingham jail because he had sought to condemn racial segregation and discrimination to audiences who hated and feared those messages.

Given officials' consistent pattern of enacting and enforcing laws to stifle civil rights advocacy, the NAACP (National Association for the Advancement of Colored People) and other leaders of the twentieth-century civil rights movement have opposed viewpoint-based censorship, including "hate speech" laws. When such laws were enacted in Skokie, Illinois, in 1977, for the specific purpose of blocking a planned neo-Nazi demonstration, the ACLU (American Civil Liberties Union), which won a Supreme Court ruling striking them down, pointed out that these laws "could have been used to stop Martin Luther King, Jr.'s confrontational march into Cicero, Illinois, in 1968."

Notably, the asserted harms that abolitionist speech was feared to cause—libel, emotional injury, and violence—are the very same harms that are now cited in support of "hate speech" laws. Accordingly, some proponents of such laws argue that they should target group libel or speech that might damage reputation or dignity;

some maintain that they should target speech that could cause emotional or psychic injury; and some contend that they should target speech that may trigger violence. If we made an exception to the viewpoint neutrality and emergency principles for "hate speech" on these rationales, that would unravel protection for today's counterparts of abolitionist and pro–civil rights speech: expression advocating racial justice that some officials and community members view as disfavored, disturbing, or feared. A prime target would include expression by the Black Lives Matter movement, which has been attacked as "hate speech" and even blamed for spurring murders of police officers. Indeed, the Southern Poverty Law Center, which monitors "hate groups," has been lobbied to designate BLM as such, and in the wake of the Charlottesville violence in August 2017 some state legislatures as well as the Republican National Committee debated decrying BLM in proposed resolutions condemning bigotry and "hate speech."

We see the same patterns concerning the movements for women's rights and reproductive freedom. Their messages advocating law reform were viewed as disfavored, disturbing, or feared from the perspective of traditional religious and cultural values, and hence censored. That is why Planned Parenthood's founding mother, Margaret Sanger, was repeatedly imprisoned. More recently, the movement for LGBT rights has depended especially strongly on robust freedom for expression that many people hated and even found hateful, as Jonathan Rauch observed in the above epigraph. After all, for LGBT individuals, the very first step toward liberation and equality is literally speaking out, "coming out of the closet," and expressly affirming their sexual orientation and gender identity. Conversely, until recently, large majorities of our society and officials perceived LGBT rights advocacy as conveying disfavored, disturbing, and feared messages, which therefore were subjected to various censorial measures.

SUPPRESSING CONSTITUTIONALLY PROTECTED
"HATE SPEECH" ON CAMPUS

"[W]e . . . should remember the long, sorry history of preventing . . .
civil rights activists from speaking at Southern universities on
grounds that they might prove 'disruptive' or 'offensive' to the campus community, not to mention the earlier exclusion of suspected
communists."

—Harvard University president Derek Bok

The venerable First Amendment principles that shelter constitutionally protected "hate speech" never have been well understood
among broad segments of the public. In fact, many people errone-
ously assume that something they call "hate speech" is absolutely
unprotected by the First Amendment. Let me cite two recent
examples, which occurred in 2017. In response to the University of
California, Berkeley's cancellation of a speaking engagement by conservative commentator Ann Coulter, former Democratic National
Committee chair and Vermont governor Howard Dean declared that
"Hate speech is not protected by the First Amendment." A month
later, in seeking to cancel two upcoming demonstrations, which he
labeled as "alt-right," Portland, Oregon mayor Ted Wheeler repeated
Dean's erroneous pronouncement verbatim.

Sadly, we have recently seen extensive speech suppression on
college and university campuses, where free speech and intellectual
freedom should be the most secure. When public universities intro-
duced "hate speech" codes in the late 1980s, they were promptly
and successfully challenged in court by the ACLU and others as
violating the First Amendment. Nonetheless, some public higher
education institutions still seek to suppress what they deem to be
"hate speech" by invoking rules that bar "harassment" and mandate
"civility."

In at least some instances current campus censorship threatens even more speech than the invalidated "hate speech" codes of the past. For example, some institutions have gone so far as to prohibit ideas that some students may find "unwelcome" or that make them "uncomfortable." Moreover, the older "hate speech" codes usually punished only personal insults that were directly addressed to a particular individual or to a small group of individuals. In contrast, today's capacious concept of "hate speech" is often understood as encompassing the expression of any idea that some students consider objectionable. In 2015, the University of Missouri Police Department (yes, the *police* department!) issued a campus-wide email instructing students to alert its officers to any "hateful or hurtful speech," pledging to investigate any such allegations and to report them to university administrators to pursue disciplinary proceedings.

Even beyond official suppression, many public colleges and universities have experienced increasing self-censorship among students and faculty about sensitive, controverted topics that urgently call for candid, vigorous debate and discussion. Given the adverse consequences at stake, there is widespread fear of being accused of "hate speech," or even of saying something that makes someone "uncomfortable," which is a damning indictment in the current campus climate.

WHY SHOULD WE SPECIALLY PROTECT SPEECH?

"Freedom of expression is not only a fundamental right but also an 'enabler' of other rights, including economic, social and cultural rights, such as the right to education and the right to take part in cultural life and to enjoy the benefits of scientific progress . . . , as well as civil and political rights. . . . [U]se of criminal law to sanction

legitimate expression constitutes one of the gravest forms of restriction . . . , as it . . . leads to other human rights violations."
—Frank LaRue, Former UN Special Rapporteur
on Freedom of Expression

"[T]he First Amendment . . . not only . . . is the lifeblood of democracy and an indispensable element of freedom, but . . . it is the guarantor of civil society itself. It protects the press, the academy, religion, political parties, and nonprofit associations."
—David Cole, ACLU Legal Director

Why shouldn't we suppress speech that conveys hateful and discriminatory ideas? Why shouldn't we try to stop those ideas from spreading, and from potentially contributing to discriminatory or violent action? And why shouldn't we try to protect the psychic well-being and dignity of the people whom the speech disparages? To be sure, constitutionally protected "hate speech" does not directly cause specific imminent serious harm; that is precisely why it may not be punished. But why isn't censorship justified by the speech's feared harmful tendency: to potentially cause emotional harm and to possibly contribute to potential future discriminatory or violent acts?

These are compelling questions, to which opponents of "hate speech" laws must provide compelling answers. That is this book's mission. This mission is especially urgent because the arguments that seek to justify "hate speech" laws are the very same arguments that always have been advanced to support restrictions on any speech whose message is disfavored, disturbing, or feared, even though it does not directly cause specific serious imminent harm. Familiar examples include speech that criticizes a war or other government policies; flag burning; speech that is said to promote terrorism or "extremism"; "fake" news; depictions of violence; speech that makes audience members feel anxious or "uncomfortable"; speech that cultural and religious conservatives find "offensive" to "traditional family values"; and sexual expression, which has been assailed for allegedly contributing to harms ranging from discrimination against women, to unplanned pregnancies among teenagers, to undermining social mores. We frequently hear calls to censor these and other types of speech because their messages are disfavored, disturbing, or feared. Therefore, by explaining why these rationales do not justify censoring constitutionally protected "hate speech," this book also makes clear why they do not justify suppressing other controversial speech.

Surveys confirm that most American adults do not know much about the First Amendment, let alone about how the Supreme Court has interpreted and applied it. Many proponents of banning constitutionally protected "hate speech" are unfamiliar with even the bedrock premise underlying the First Amendment: that speech, in contrast with "nonverbal conduct," has special value.

Freedom of speech has been a long and widely cherished right for multiple reasons, venerated under international human rights law and in most national legal systems. For individuals, it is essential for forming and communicating thoughts, as well as for expressing emotions. It is a prerequisite for democratic self-government in the United States, allowing "We the People" to exchange information and opinions with each other, and with our elected officials, in order to influence policy and to hold officials accountable. Additionally, freedom of speech is the prerequisite for exercising all other rights and freedoms, enabling us to advocate and organize in support of such rights, and to petition the government for redress of rights violations. Free speech also facilitates the search for truth and promotes tolerance. Speaking from his prison cell in 2010, upon having been awarded the Nobel Peace Prize, Chinese human rights activist Liu Xiaobo eloquently described this precious freedom, for which he had sacrificed his physical liberty: "Free expression is the foundation of human rights, the source of humanity, and the mother of truth."

Many Supreme Court justices have eloquently captured the many interrelated benefits of freedom of speech, for both liberty and equality, in opinions supporting freedom even for speech whose messages were disfavored, disturbing, or feared. In fact, Supreme Court opinions about freedom of speech inevitably concern speech with such messages; otherwise, the speech would not have been subject to the restrictions that prompted the constitutional challenges. Some of these opinions have involved "hate speech"; even more have involved pro–civil rights advocacy—which, in many parts of the United States, and for much of our history, has been regarded as disfavored, disturbing, and feared.

Counterbalanced against the special values of speech, in contrast with other, "nonverbal," conduct, is speech's reduced, indirect, and unpredictable role in fostering harm. Like other forms of conduct, one person's speech can, of course, affect other people. Speech can affect listeners' emotions, psyches, beliefs, and behavior. Unlike other forms of conduct, though, speech can influence listeners only through their intermediating perceptions, reactions, and actions, and only as one of countless other factors that also have potential influence. For this reason, hurling words at someone is materially different from hurling the proverbial "sticks and stones." Sticks and stones directly cause harm, through their own force, but words at most can potentially contribute to harm; whether particular words actually do cause harm depends on how individual listeners perceive and respond to them, which in turn is influenced by the listeners' personalities and circumstances, including innumerable other factors that also potentially influence their psyches and behavior.

In sum, speech has both an enhanced positive value and a reduced negative potential when contrasted with most forms of conduct, and thus warrants special protection.

THE AMERICAN APPROACH HAS BEEN CHAMPIONED
BY CITIZENS OF MANY OTHER COUNTRIES

"[I]nternational law on insulting speech should be applied in a manner that is . . . more protective of speech, in line with the approach espoused by the U.S. Supreme Court under the First Amendment. . . . Intent to incite hatred, hostility or discrimination should be insufficient to justify criminal sanctions."
—Amal Clooney and Philippa Webb,
British human rights barristers

"[T]he American way of dealing with Nazism . . . always seemed to me the more mature way of handling threats to liberal democracy. Germany's [outlawing of "hate speech"] seems like a permanent declaration of distrust in . . . argument and . . . education. . . . I have faith in a democratic public's ability to police itself. I wish Germany did."
—Anna Sauerbrey, editor of German newspaper
Der Tagesspiegel

"Hate speech" laws undermine universal principles of liberty, equality, and democracy. Thus, the case against such laws does not rest only on the text of the First Amendment or on the Supreme Court's interpretations of that guarantee. On the other hand, when the same general principles are applied in different contexts, they may lead to different outcomes. For example, "hate speech" that does not pose an imminent danger of inciting violence in one country might do so in another.

I hope that the general principles I advocate in this book will at least be thoroughly considered by those who seek to advance both free speech and equality elsewhere in the world. Indeed, it is noteworthy that the American approach to these issues has been championed by human rights advocates, lawyers, and other experts in international agencies and in many other countries. These international supporters of the American approach have witnessed first-hand the actual impact of "hate speech" laws in other countries, concluding that, no matter how well intentioned, these laws have been detrimental in practice. Here are just a few recent examples of pertinent statements from these many worldwide "hate speech" law critics.

- In 2017, the European Centre for Press and Media Freedom (ECPMF), based in Germany, issued a statement opposing proposed German legislation requiring social media to block or remove "hate speech," explaining: "Combating illegal incitement to violence, hatred, . . . and discrimination is indeed . . . crucial. . . . But . . . censoring speech has never [been] shown to be effective: it is rather by more speech . . . that our societies will be helped."
- In 2017, a racially diverse coalition of prominent South African comedians and satirists called for limiting that country's "hate speech" laws to essentially track the American approach. The coalition members expressed concern about the laws' censorial impact on humor, including political humor.
- In 2015, the European Commission Against Racism and Intolerance (ECRI) issued a report critiquing European "hate speech" laws as insufficiently effective and potentially even counterproductive; the report urged European countries to prioritize non-censorial alternative measures, including counterspeech, concluding that they were "much more likely" than censorship "to prove effective in ultimately eradicating" "hate speech" and its potential harmful effects.
- In 2015, UNESCO (United Nations Educational, Scientific and Cultural Organization) issued a report on "Countering Online Hate Speech," which stressed that "Counter-speech is generally preferable to suppression of speech."

- Even the committee that enforces the UN's International Convention on the Elimination of All Forms of Racial Discrimination (CERD), which went into effect in 1969, and requires ratifying countries to enact "hate speech" laws, in 2013 downplayed the enforcement of such laws and instead stressed the importance of "education for tolerance, and counter-speech. . . [as] effective antidotes to racist hate speech."

The foregoing are just a handful of the many similar critiques I could cite. In his 2016 book that endorsed the American position, Oxford University professor Timothy Garton Ash wrote: "[S]ome British human rights activists . . . privately acknowledge the need to amend if not repeal Britain's law on incitement to racial hatred, on . . . grounds of equal treatment, but few will say this publicly." Ash's observation underscores the key point that "hate speech" laws undermine equality, as well as free speech. After he wrote that passage, two prominent British human rights barristers publicly called for repealing "hate speech" laws in Britain and elsewhere in a 2017 article in the *Columbia Human Rights Law Review* that I quoted above.

"HATE SPEECH" LAWS LONG WERE OPPOSED BY OTHER DEMOCRATIC COUNTRIES

Many proponents of "hate speech" laws would probably be surprised to learn that these laws were initially promoted in the then-new United Nations by the Soviet Union and its allies, and that such laws were staunchly opposed by almost all liberal democracies. The Soviet Union persistently pushed for language permitting or even requiring UN member states to restrict "hate speech" in meetings of the UN bodies that worked on the Universal Declaration of Human Rights and other major UN instruments. The proposed language was closely modeled on the constitutions of the communist regimes. For example, the Soviet Union's 1936 constitution provided that "Any advocacy of racial or national . . . hatred . . . is punishable by law."

Eleanor Roosevelt, who was the U.S. representative to the UN from 1946 to 1953, warned that incorporating such language in UN instruments was "extremely dangerous" and "likely to be exploited by totalitarian States for the purpose of rendering the other [human rights] articles null and void," because "criticism of public or religious authorities might all too easily be described as incitement to hatred and consequently prohibited." Likewise, representatives of other democratic countries maintained that "hate speech" laws could be invoked "to suppress the opinions of opposition groups and parties." These warnings proved sadly prophetic: the communist proponents of such laws did regularly enforce them to suppress speech by political dissidents as well as by ethnic and religious minorities. Current advocates of "hate speech" laws regularly criticize American "exceptionalism" on this issue, but for several decades the American position was shared by most other countries that also shared our democratic political system and support for free expression.

Of course, the merits of "hate speech" laws do not depend on how popular or unpopular they are around the world. Nonetheless, it is noteworthy that, for a substantial period, so many democratic countries resisted substantial pressure to support these laws, citing reasons that many of their citizens continue to cite to this day.

THE ANTI-DEMOCRATIC ENFORCEMENT OF "HATE SPEECH" LAWS EVEN IN DEMOCRACIES

"[T]o see what the actual rather than the hoped-for effects of hate speech laws are . . . [j]ust look at how such laws in Europe are now

being applied, and against whom. Who could possibly look at that
and view it as desirable?"

—Journalist Glenn Greenwald

The major advocates of "hate speech" laws in the United States
maintain that such laws should punish only individually targeted
insults, not general statements about social and political issues. Yet
these laws often have been used in other democracies to investigate,
prosecute, and penalize expressions of ideas about pressing public
policy issues, even by political candidates and officials. Equally dismaying, they often have been used to punish Christian and Muslim
members of the clergy for quoting the Bible and the Qur'an, including during religious services in their houses of worship. Such censorship is the predictable result of granting government officials the
discretion that "hate speech" laws inevitably bestow.

To illustrate what we could expect under "hate speech" laws in
the United States, below is just a sampling of the expression that
recently has been targeted under such laws in other democratic
countries. (Later chapters provide many additional examples.)

- In 2017, two British street preachers were convicted for preaching
  from the Bible, including statements that were deemed insulting
  to LGBT persons and Muslims. The prosecutor told the Court:
  "[A]lthough the words preached are included in a version of the
  Bible in 1611, this does not mean that they are not capable of
  amounting to a [criminal] offense in 2016."
- In 2016, a Danish appellate court affirmed a lower court's conviction of a man who had posted Facebook comments criticizing
  "[t]he ideology of Islam," charging that "Islam wants to abuse
  democracy in order to get rid of democracy."
- In 2016, Laure Pora, who headed the Paris chapter of the LGBT
  rights organization ACT-UP, was fined €2,300 for applying the

term "homophobe" to Ludovine de La Rochère, the president of an organization that defends "traditional family values" and opposes same-sex marriage; ACT-UP activists had posted flyers featuring de La Rochère with the word "homophobe" over her face.

- In 2015, France's highest court upheld criminal convictions and fines totaling $14,500 for twelve pro-Palestinian activists who went to supermarkets wearing T-shirts with the message "Long live Palestine, boycott Israel," and handed out flyers that said "buying Israeli products means legitimizing crimes in Gaza."

- In 2014, a British church was sanctioned for displaying a sign on its property showing burning flames and stating, "If you think there is no God you better be right!!"

- In 2013, a Catholic bishop in Switzerland was subject to a criminal complaint and investigation for quoting Old Testament passages about homosexuality during a debate on marriage and the family.

- In 2011, an Australian journalist and his newspaper employer were convicted because of his columns complaining that "there are fair-skinned people in Australia with essentially European ancestry . . . who, motivated by career opportunities available to Aboriginal people or by political activism, have chosen to falsely identify as Aboriginal."

- In 2010, a Danish historian and journalist was convicted for saying during an interview that there was a high crime rate in areas with high Muslim populations.

- In 2010, Polish police criminally charged two singers because of critical statements they made about the Bible and the Catholic Church. One had said that the Bible was "unbelievable" and had been written by people "drunk on wine and smoking some kind of herbs." The other allegedly said, during a performance, that the Catholic Church was "the most murderous cult on the planet," and he tore up a copy of the Bible.

- In 2009, an Austrian Member of Parliament was convicted, sentenced to a prison term (which was suspended), and fined €24,000 because she said that "in today's system" Muhammad would be considered a child molester, since his wife Aisha was believed to be around 6 or 7 years old when they were married and 9 years old when they consummated the marriage.

- In 2008, a 15-year-old British boy was charged by police and investigated by prosecutors because he displayed a sign during a peaceful demonstration reading: "Scientology is not a religion, it is a dangerous cult."

- In 2008, the Canadian weekly magazine *Maclean's* was subjected to proceedings before multiple enforcement bodies because articles it had published were allegedly Islamophobic.

- In 2008, Brigitte Bardot, French former film star and longtime animal rights activist, was convicted and fined €15,000 for writing a letter to then–Interior Minister Nicolas Sarkozy complaining about Muslims' ritual slaughter of sheep and stating that Muslims are "destroying our country by imposing their ways."

- In 2005, the French newspaper *Le Monde* was found guilty of inciting hatred against Jews because of a 2002 editorial that criticized certain Israeli policies while referring to Israel as "a nation of refugees."

- In 2001, a Dutch imam was prosecuted because he said during a national TV interview that homosexual behavior was "detrimental to Dutch society" and an "infectious disease," citing the Qu'ran and other Muslim texts.

- In 1999, Britain's then–Home Secretary Jack Straw was subjected to a formal investigation for inciting racial hatred against the Roma because he had said that some criminal activity was carried out by people who posed as "gypsies" or "travelers."

PRIVATE-SECTOR INSTITUTIONS SHOULD PROTECT
FREE SPEECH

"[Social media] platforms—although not formally bound by the First Amendment—have a democratic obligation to embrace something close to the constitutional standard. . . . Like universities and media outlets, online speech platforms should not be safe spaces. They should be democratic spaces, with the ultimate victors in the clash of ideas determined by reason and deliberation . . ."
—George Washington University law professor Jeffrey Rosen

"I woke up in a bad mood and decided [the *Daily Stormer*] shouldn't be allowed on the Internet. No one should have that power. [A Cloudflare employee] asked after I told him [about this decision]: 'Is this the day the Internet dies?'"
—Matthew Prince, CEO of Cloudflare

I concur with Jeffrey Rosen and Matthew Prince that certain powerful private-sector actors, which are not directly subject to constitutional constraints because they are not part of the government, should nonetheless respect the free speech rights of others over whom they exercise power. This is most important for private-sector entities that are engaged in communications activities, and that in turn affect the communications opportunities of others. Prime examples are private universities and online intermediaries, including internet service providers, search engines, and social media platforms. In general, they should hesitate to bar any expression that government could not bar, including constitutionally protected "hate speech."

I use the qualifying phrase "in general," because particular private institutions may opt to implement different standards to advance other values they deem paramount. Doing this is consistent with their own constitutional rights. For example, private universities that are affiliated with particular religious denominations could opt to bar certain speech that is inconsistent with their religious beliefs. They should provide clear advance notice of any such policies, so that any potential students, faculty members, and others could make informed decisions about whether or not to become associated with those universities.

Likewise, a particular online platform could choose to create a certain environment, to appeal to a specific segment of the public, including through viewpoint-based restrictions on expression that participants may post and access. For example, the Misscliks channel on the videogame streaming platform Twitch was founded in 2013, when gamer culture was criticized for being misogynistic, as "a place where people of all genders and backgrounds could participate in gamer culture without fear, prejudice, or harassment." Toward that end, Misscliks takes various steps to curb sexist or misogynistic comments, including banning outright people who persistently make such comments.

In light of the enormous power of private universities and online intermediaries either to facilitate or stifle the free exchange of ideas and information, I would urge that, except in unusual circumstances, they should permit all expression that the First Amendment shields from government censorship. The Supreme Court hailed the unique importance of online intermediaries in this regard in a unanimous 2017 ruling that recognized "cyberspace . . . and social media in particular" as "the most important places . . . for the exchange of views," serving "for many" people as "the principal" means for doing so.

Most private universities do pledge to honor free speech principles, as consistent with academic freedom and sound pedagogy, although they do not always live up to that commitment. The online situation is more problematic. In a July 2017 article entitled "Facebook Struggles in Fighting Hate Speech," the *Washington Post* observed that "[l]ike most [American] social media companies . . . , Facebook . . . long resisted being a gatekeeper for speech," with its CEO Marc Zuckerberg reiterating that it was "a tech company, not a media company." The *Post* chronicled Facebook's recent shift, reflected in Zuckerberg's June 2017 announcement of the company's revised mission statement, embracing the goals of "keeping us safe" and "inclusion of all." In a 2017 story about Facebook's enforcement of its internal standards proscribing "hate speech" and other disfavored messages, the *Guardian* aptly observed that Facebook is "de facto . . . the world's largest censor." Susan Benesch, director of the Dangerous Speech Project, added that "Facebook is regulating more . . . speech than any government . . . ever has." Later that year, Facebook said that it "now deletes about 288,000 hate-speech posts a month."

Granted, online intermediaries that operate internationally must comply with laws in other countries that are less speech-protective than the United States, including "hate speech" laws. Even so, the online companies can opt for "geo-blocking," confining the restrictive measures to the pertinent geographical territory. In short, to the maximum extent feasible, these important institutions should wield their vast power consistent with the core speech-protective viewpoint neutrality and emergency principles. When they do not do so, there are serious downsides for free speech, democracy, and equality. In Chapters 4 and 7, I offer some examples of these problems.

Since the very first U.S. federal law regulating the internet, Congress has wisely encouraged online intermediaries to serve as open conduits for the free-flowing exchange of ideas and information. The 1996 Communications Decency Act broadly shields online intermediaries from liability for material that others distribute (with some exceptions). It thus incentivizes online platforms to serve as "common carriers" for the communications of others, without suppressing any such communications due solely to their disfavored, disturbing, or feared messages. This is the same important role that the landline telephone system long has played. In contrast, other governments, as well as some international bodies, have imposed speech-suppressive regulations on online intermediaries that operate within their jurisdictions, including by requiring them to bar what would be constitutionally protected "hate speech" in the United States.

In order to foster freedom of expression in the increasingly important online realm, many international agencies and human rights organizations have urged that online intermediaries should facilitate free speech, and resist censorship, in two major ways: governments should not impose speech-regulating functions upon such intermediaries; and the intermediaries should not be liable for third-party content (the situation in the United States described above). For example, in a 2017 Joint Declaration, the free expression experts of the UN, the Organization for Security and Cooperation in Europe, the Organization of American States, and the African Commission on Human and Peoples' Rights criticized "attempts by some governments to suppress dissent and to control public communications . . . by pressuring intermediaries to . . . restrict [online] content."

This book focuses primarily on government action, rather than on private online intermediaries and other private entities, which are not governed by the First Amendment. Nonetheless, I want to register my view—which is shared by many experts—that certain private institutions, including universities and online intermediaries, should not suppress constitutionally protected "hate speech" in light of the principled and policy concerns that I set out in this book, in explaining why government should not do so.

NON-CENSORIAL STRATEGIES

"The strategic response to hate speech is more speech: more speech that educates about cultural differences; more speech that promotes diversity; more speech to empower and give voice to minorities. . . . More speech can be the best way to reach out to individuals, changing what they think and not merely what they do."
—2011 UN Expert Workshop on the Prohibition of National, Racial, or Religious Hatred

Substantial evidence demonstrates that the counterspeech strategy is at least as effective as censorship, not only in checking the potentially adverse effects of constitutionally protected "hate speech," but also in promoting the dignity and empowerment of the individuals and groups the speech targets. We must focus on deterring discriminatory attitudes and conduct. Censoring constitutionally protected "hate speech" is a superficial and cheap "quick fix" that not only fails to actually fix these problems, but also tends to divert attention and resources from more effective measures. For this reason, some former advocates of the initial campus "hate speech" codes in the late 1980s and early 1990s became disillusioned with them. For this same reason, human rights activists in many countries, and in international organizations, are increasingly prioritizing non-censorial alternatives.

While he was president, Barack Obama repeatedly endorsed the "more speech" approach, from his perspective as the frequent target of hateful speech and as a champion of equality and inclusivity. Supporting strong freedom of speech on campus even for "language that is offensive to African Americans or . . . sends a demeaning signal towards women," Obama explained to student audiences that "being . . . an activist . . . involves hearing the other side and . . . engaging in a dialogue because that's . . . how change happens." He cited the civil rights movement as exemplifying this approach, stating that it "happened because . . . the leadership . . . consistently . . . sought to understand the views" of their opponents, "even views that were appalling to them." Urging students to "have an argument with" those whose views they reject, he insisted that "[y]ou shouldn't silence anyone by saying . . . 'I'm too sensitive to hear what you have to say.'"

Although acknowledging that it would be especially burdensome to minority students and other disparaged people to answer back, Obama recognized that this effort is an essential, empowering step toward the social justice reforms they champion: "[Y]es, [this] . . . may put a slightly higher burden on [such students]. But you're not going to make the kinds of deep changes in society that those students want, without taking . . . on [their opponents] in a . . . courageous way."

COST–BENEFIT ANALYSIS OF "HATE SPEECH" LAWS

To fairly evaluate the arguments for and against "hate speech" laws, we must first understand the pertinent First Amendment principles about when "hate speech" is punishable and when it is protected, and the important reasons for the distinction. The issue is usually falsely framed as *whether* American law should punish "hate speech." In fact, the actual issue is, rather, whether there are *some* circumstances in which "hate speech" should be punished and, in particular, whether it should be punished in circumstances beyond those in which it *already* is punishable.

On the one hand, what would we gain by censoring constitutionally protected "hate speech"? Would this censorship reduce the potential harms to which such speech is feared to contribute: discrimination, violence, and psychic harms? On the other hand, what would we lose by censoring such speech? What would be the costs to freedom of speech and democratic self-government? Would there be adverse impacts on the goals of reducing discrimination, violence, and psychic harms? Are there alternative methods for effectively pursuing these goals?

The analysis of the foregoing questions, in the chapters that follow, demonstrates that the costs of "hate speech" laws would outweigh the benefits, and that the desired benefits can be effectively promoted through non-censorial alternatives. The following chapters support several, independently sufficient, grounds for reaching these conclusions:

1. There is insufficient evidence that constitutionally protected "hate speech" (as distinguished from "hate speech" that is already punishable) materially contributes to the harms that are said to warrant its suppression.
2. Even if there were sufficient evidence that constitutionally protected "hate speech" did materially contribute to these feared harms, "hate speech" laws would not effectively reduce the feared harms.
3. Even if there were sufficient evidence that constitutionally protected "hate speech" did materially contribute to the feared harms, and even if "hate speech" laws would meaningfully reduce these feared harms, these laws should still be rejected because of the damage they would do to freedom of speech and democratic legitimacy, as well as to equality and societal harmony.

The preceding points are developed more fully in the chapters that follow. I hope that my analysis will generate not only thought, discussion, and debate, but also advocacy and action to advance all of the important concerns at issue: individual liberty and equality, freedom of expression, democratic self-government, societal harmony, and psychic well-being.

CHAPTER TWO

"Hate Speech" Laws Violate Fundamental Free Speech and Equality Principles

As ALREADY NOTED, all "hate speech" laws, no matter how they are drafted, inherently violate the emergency and viewpoint neutrality principles. In this chapter, I explain why those principles are so important, especially for minority views and voices, thus illuminating the damage that "hate speech" laws would inflict on both liberty and equality. I next explore the reasons why the Supreme Court has allowed the government to restrict certain other categories of speech, explaining why the rationales for those decisions do not apply to constitutionally protected "hate speech." Finally, I explain both why "hate speech" laws are more problematic than speech regulations that are constitutionally permissible, and why authorizing government to enact "hate speech" laws would unleash government's power to suppress any speech whose message is disfavored, disturbing, or feared.

THE VIEWPOINT NEUTRALITY AND EMERGENCY
PRINCIPLES: TWIN PILLARS OF LIBERTY AND EQUALITY

"If there is a bedrock principle underlying the First Amendment, it is that the government may not prohibit the expression of an idea simply because society finds the idea itself offensive or disagreeable. . . . The First Amendment does not guarantee that concepts virtually sacred to our Nation as a whole—such as the principle that discrimination on the basis of race is odious and destructive—will go unquestioned in the marketplace of ideas."
—Justice William Brennan, *Texas v. Johnson* (1989)

"[N]o danger flowing from speech can be deemed clear and present, unless the incidence of the evil apprehended is so imminent that it may befall before there is opportunity for full discussion. If there be time to expose through discussion the falsehood and fallacies, . . . the remedy . . . is more speech, not enforced silence. Only an emergency can justify repression."
—Justice Louis Brandeis, *Whitney v. California* (1927)

Together, the core viewpoint neutrality and emergency principles bar government from regulating speech solely because its message is disfavored, disturbing, or feared. Instead, these complementary principles permit government to regulate speech only when necessary to avert an emergency because it directly causes specific imminent serious harm.

An important 1972 decision, *Chicago v. Mosley*, illustrates how essential these principles are for speech challenging the status quo and advocating equality. The Court's opinion was written by Justice Thurgood Marshall. The first African American to serve on the high Court, Marshall is best known for his trailblazing advocacy on behalf of racial justice, including as one of the NAACP lawyers who litigated the landmark *Brown v. Board of Education* school desegregation case. Marshall also is celebrated as a champion of First

Amendment freedoms. Because these freedoms were essential for the civil rights movement, Marshall's stalwart support of free speech is hardly coincidental.

Like so many key free speech rulings, *Mosley* upheld the freedom of speech for a pro–civil rights message and for a speaker who was a member of a racial minority. Specifically, it protected the right of Earl Mosley, an African-American postal employee, to continue peacefully picketing on public sidewalks near Jones Commercial High School in Chicago. He had been carrying a sign reading "Jones High School practices black discrimination. Jones High School has a black quota."

Just as freedom of speech has been a constant ally of the civil rights struggle, censorship has been its constant foe. In the *Mosley* case, as in so many others, the government sought to stifle a pro–civil rights message. In this instance, Chicago had enacted a new ordinance that outlawed any picketing near a public school, unless the picketing related to a labor dispute affecting the school. The Chicago Police Department warned Mosley that if he continued to picket, he would be arrested.

In striking down the new law, because of its discrimination among messages and speakers, Justice Marshall emphasized the mutually reinforcing principles of equality and liberty:

> [A]bove all else, the First Amendment means that government has no power to restrict expression because of its message, its ideas, its subject matter, or its content . . . [G]overnment may not grant the use of a forum to people whose views it finds acceptable, but deny use to those wishing to express less favored or more controversial views. There is an "equality of status in the field of ideas," and government must afford all points of view an equal opportunity to be heard.

If we empowered government to enforce "hate speech" laws, eviscerating the hard-won viewpoint neutrality and emergency principles, we would be rolling back the clock to an earlier period in our history, when government punished speech because of its feared harmful tendency. In the next section, I describe how the now-discredited bad tendency test operated as a license to suppress any speech with a disfavored, disturbing, or feared message, to underscore that reinstating it would be especially damaging to dissenting views.

THE HARMFUL IMPACT OF THE BAD TENDENCY TEST

Until the second half of the twentieth century, the Supreme Court enforced the deferential "bad tendency" standard to permit government to suppress speech whenever it maintained that the speech might cause harm at some future point. Under this standard, for example, in a series of decisions in 1919, the Court upheld criminal convictions for speech opposing U.S. involvement in World War I, on the rationale that the speech might induce some individuals to resist military service, which might in turn harm our national interests. Authorizing the government to punish speech based on such an attenuated, speculative connection between the speech and potential harm enabled the government to engage in rampant viewpoint discrimination, essentially silencing all dissent against its policies concerning the war or the draft.

In *Debs v. United States*, for example, the bad tendency test was applied to uphold the conviction of Socialist Party leader Eugene V. Debs, who had received 6% of the national vote in his 1912 U.S. presidential campaign, because he gave a wartime speech that criticized the draft. As we will see in Chapter 4, one of the most dismaying impacts of "hate speech" laws in other democratic countries is their regular enforcement against politicians for similar kinds of statements, criticizing government policies. As Justice Louis

Brandeis later observed in opposing the bad tendency test, "Every denunciation of existing law tends in some measure to increase the probability that there will be violation of it." Indeed, it was precisely this rationale that prompted the censorship and imprisonment of Margaret Sanger and other pioneering birth-control advocates, who criticized laws that criminalized the use of contraception.

In the 1919 *Abrams* case, Justice Holmes, joined by Justice Brandeis, repudiated the bad tendency test in a powerful dissenting opinion, declaring that the First Amendment bars government from suppressing even "opinions that we loathe" and "believe to be fraught with death," unless they "so imminently threaten immediate interference" with national interests "that an immediate check is required to save the country."

"HATE SPEECH" LAWS UNDERMINE EQUAL RIGHTS MOVEMENTS

"Without freedom of speech and the right to dissent, the Civil Rights movement would have been a bird without wings."
—Congressman John Lewis

Equal rights advocates have always been dependent on a vigorous concept of free speech, including the viewpoint neutrality and emergency principles, because their views are often regarded as disfavored, disturbing, and feared, and therefore targeted for censorship. In Chapter 1, I described multiple illustrations of this pattern in the United States, and in Chapter 4 I will offer examples from other countries as well. Here, though, I want to take note of one especially salient historic episode in the United States: the twentieth-century civil rights movement. In his book *Hate Speech: The History of an American Controversy*, historian Samuel Walker documents the opposition to "hate speech" laws by major civil rights organizations, including the NAACP, the American Jewish Congress, and the American Jewish Committee.

The opposition by the first two groups is especially noteworthy because both had initially supported such laws. Their about-faces reflected their experience with hostile government officials who employed a wide array of speech regulations in efforts to suppress their antidiscrimination advocacy. Based on their experience, these civil rights groups came to recognize that any speech regulations that did not conform to the viewpoint neutrality and emergency principles, including "hate speech" laws, could likewise be turned against them. After all, well into the second half of the twentieth century pro–civil rights advocacy was widely feared as subverting traditional societal institutions and law and order. It is no coincidence that the movement's leaders were demonized as communists, probably the most hated and feared group at the time, whose expression also was widely suppressed because of its feared harmful tendency. In the words of University of Chicago law professor Harry Kalven, "the NAACP is from the standpoint of the beleaguered South a second domestic conspiracy aiming at a revolution."

CONSTITUTIONALLY PROTECTED "HATE SPEECH" IS NOT
INCLUDED IN THE CATEGORIES OF SPEECH THAT THE COURT
HAS HELD TO BE UNPROTECTED BY THE FIRST AMENDMENT

The Supreme Court has recognized a "few," "narrowly limited," and shrinking sets of "historic and traditional categories" of speech, defined by their messages, which it has deemed to be outside the core of the First Amendment's protection due to their "low value," thus not furthering the First Amendment's central purposes. In the past, these categories have included defamation, commercial advertising, obscenity, and fighting words. Since the 1960s, the Court has substantially narrowed both the list of such unprotected categories of expression and their definitions. Moreover, in a landmark 2010 decision, the Court decreed that it henceforth would not "carve out from the First Amendment any novel" additional categories of unprotected speech.

Whatever the merits of this "low value" doctrine, which has always been controversial, it never has applied to "hate speech." To the contrary, "hate speech" constitutes political speech, which the Court always has regarded as having uniquely high value, therefore being entitled to full First Amendment protection, even if the public might "despise" its message. The Court has consistently held that the First Amendment protects political speech that it has characterized with a wide variety of negative or critical adjectives, including "contemptuous," "controversial," "disagreeable," "distasteful," "hurtful," "inappropriate," "indecent," "insulting," "misguided," "offensive," "opprobrious," "outrageous," "patently offensive," "provocative," "scurrilous," "shocking," "unsettling," "upsetting," and "vulgar."

There is another fundamental reason why constitutionally protected "hate speech" cannot be considered of low value: such speech not only addresses public policy issues, but it also conveys specific viewpoints about them. The Court repeatedly has stressed that a speech regulation that "curtail[s] expression of a particular point of view on controversial issues of general interest is the purest example" of a law that violates the First Amendment.

In an important, highly pertinent 2017 decision, *Matal v. Tam*, the Court explained that the viewpoint neutrality principle specifically "protects the right to . . . present arguments for particular positions in particular ways, as the speaker chooses," expressly noting that "[g]iving offense is a viewpoint," which accordingly may not be suppressed. In *Matal*, the Court unanimously enforced these precepts to strike down a federal statute that was, in effect, a "hate speech" law. Using key terms that many "hate speech" laws contain, this statute barred trademarks that "disparage" any persons "or bring [them] into contempt or disrepute." Moreover, the government maintained that the statute's purpose was to protect members of minority groups from being subjected to "demeaning messages," which is also the purpose of "hate speech" laws. Under this statute, the government had refused to register as a trademark a term that traditionally has been used as an epithet against people of Asian ethnicity: "slants." Simon Tam, lead singer of an Asian-American rock group, "The Slants," had chosen that name in order to "reclaim" the term and "drain it of its denigrating force." In holding the statute unconstitutional, the Court explained why no "hate speech" law can pass First Amendment muster, quoting Justice Oliver Wendell Holmes's famous formulation of the viewpoint neutrality principle: "Speech that demeans on the basis of race, ethnicity, gender, religion, age, disability, or any other similar ground is hateful; but the proudest boast of our free speech jurisprudence is that we protect the freedom to express 'the thought that we hate.'"

GOVERNMENT MAY NOT PUNISH "HATE SPEECH" TO PROTECT GROUP REPUTATION OR DIGNITY

Some proponents of "hate speech" laws invoke the concept of group defamation, on the theory that constitutionally protected "hate speech," like defamation, is false and harms the reputations and dignity of individuals who belong to the disparaged groups. As its label signals, group defamation refers to speech that defames a broad group rather than particular individuals.

In the 1952 case of *Beauharnais v. Illinois*, by a 5–4 vote, the Supreme Court narrowly rejected a First Amendment challenge to an

Illinois group defamation statute. It had been enforced against someone who was circulating a petition addressed to the Chicago mayor and city council, protesting racial integration and making derogatory statements about African Americans. The Illinois Supreme Court had construed the statute as being limited to statements that had a "strong tendency . . . to cause violence and disorder." The Supreme Court held that the government could punish such statements consistent with the then-prevailing bad tendency test.

Since *Beauharnais*, the Supreme Court never has explicitly revisited the group defamation issue, but federal judges, as well as other experts, concur that the Court has implicitly overruled *Beauharnais* in a long series of subsequent decisions that have rejected its rationales. One of these was the Court's landmark 1964 decision in *New York Times v. Sullivan*, which made clear that the First Amendment strictly limits defamation lawsuits even by individuals. In *Sullivan* and subsequent cases, the Court has held that the expression at issue must constitute false statements of fact rather than opinions, and when the expression addresses matters of public concern, defamation plaintiffs bear a heavy burden of proof. Moreover, the Court has treated *Beauharnais* as a case about averting potential violence, underscoring that its holding is at odds with the emergency standard.

If government officials instead sought to justify a "hate speech" law on the traditional defamation rationale of protecting disparaged individuals and groups from reputational and dignitary harms, such a law also would violate longstanding First Amendment principles. Statements about groups involve generalizations, making them more akin to expressions of opinion than to the false statements of fact that constitute a prerequisite for a defamation claim. As the Court observed, "There is no such thing as a false idea." Moreover, even false statements of fact can't be punished except in strictly limited circumstances, when they directly inflict specific serious injury, such as defaming a particular individual or defrauding someone. As Justice Robert Jackson declared: "The very purpose of the First Amendment is to foreclose public authority from assuming a guardianship of the public mind. . . . [E]very person must be his own watchman for truth, because the forefathers did not trust any government to separate the true from the false for us."

In addition to violating fundamental free speech principles, group defamation actions would also endanger speech supporting equality causes. Justice William O. Douglas, a staunch civil rights champion, made this point in his *Beauharnais* dissent:

Today a white man stands convicted for protesting in unseemly language against our decisions invalidating [racially] restrictive covenants. Tomorrow a Negro will be hailed before a court for denouncing a lynch law in heated terms. Farm laborers in the West who compete with field hands drifting up from Mexico, . . . a minority which finds employment going to members of the dominant religious group—all of these are caught in the mesh of today's decision. . . . It is a warning to every minority.

GOVERNMENT MAY NOT PUNISH THE EXPRESSION
OF POLITICAL IDEAS, INCLUDING "HATE SPEECH,"
BECAUSE SUCH EXPRESSION MIGHT CAUSE
EMOTIONAL OR PSYCHIC HARM

"It would be grossly insensitive to deny, as we do not, that the proposed demonstration would seriously disturb, emotionally and mentally, at least some, and probably many of [Skokie's] residents. The problem with engrafting an exception on the First Amendment for such situations is that they are indistinguishable in principle from speech that 'invite(s) dispute, . . . induces a condition of unrest, creates dissatisfaction with conditions as they are, or even stirs people to anger.' . . . Yet these are among the 'high purposes' of the First Amendment."

—U.S. Court of Appeals for the Seventh Circuit,
upholding rights of neo-Nazis to demonstrate in Skokie,
Illinois (quoting U.S. Supreme Court)

Some proponents of "hate speech" laws stress the psychic or emotional harm that such speech can cause. As I relate in Chapter 6, social scientists concur that it is difficult to pinpoint the contributory role of any speech, including constitutionally protected "hate speech," to these kinds of harms. Beyond that, though, the First Amendment in principle bars government from punishing any political speech, including constitutionally protected "hate speech," on the ground that it might cause emotional or psychic harm. Instead, we must counter any potential negative emotional or psychic impact of such speech with non-censorial measures. Fortunately, as I show in Chapter 8, there is encouraging evidence that these kinds of measures can be effective. In fact, some psychologists believe that, in at least some cases, mental health might even benefit from exposure to constitutionally protected "hate speech," whereas it might actually be undermined by censorship.

The bar on punishing constitutionally protected "hate speech" because it might cause emotional or psychic harms flows from the central viewpoint neutrality principle. Any adverse emotional or psychic impact that speech might have on an audience member necessarily would result directly from "its message, its ideas, its subject matter, or its content"—factors that never justify censorship, as the Supreme Court unanimously explained in *Mosley*. Therefore, the Court has held that no civil lawsuit seeking damages for the tort of "intentional infliction of emotional distress" may be based on expression about matters of public concern, including specifically constitutionally protected "hate speech."

"If any philosophy should be regarded as completely unaccept-able to civilized society, that of plaintiffs [American neo-Nazis], who . . . have . . . deliberately identified themselves with a regime whose record of brutality and barbarism is unmatched in modern history, would be a good place to start. But there can be no legiti-mate start down such a road."

—U.S. Circuit Court of Appeals for the Seventh Circuit,
Skokie case

I hope I have persuaded you that the viewpoint neutrality and emer-gency principles are essential for protecting controversial expression, and in particular dissenting views. If so, then the only remaining issue is whether we should—or could—make a special exception for constitutionally protected "hate speech."

If these fundamental free speech principles were breached for "hate speech" laws, it would be impossible, as a matter of both prin-ciple and practicality, to continue to enforce them to protect other controversial expression. The Supreme Court stressed both of these concerns in its 1971 decision in *Cohen v. California*, in which it barred a state from suppressing what the state argued to be a uniquely odious epithet. The Court explained that "the principle contended for . . . seems inherently boundless. How is one to distinguish this [word] from any other offensive word? . . . [N]o readily ascertain-able general principle exists for stopping short of" making "public debate . . . palatable to" all of us. As the Court recognized in *Cohen*, "the immediate consequence of" our robust freedom even for hateful speech "may often appear to be only verbal tumult, discord, and even offensive utterance." It then went on to explain the net gain, for all of us as individuals, and for our society overall, from this vibrant discourse, including its disfavored, disturbing, and feared messages:

> The constitutional right of free expression is powerful medicine in a society as diverse . . . as ours. It is designed . . . to remove governmental restraints from the arena of public discussion, putting the decision as to what views shall be voiced largely into the hands of each of us, in the hope that . . . such freedom will ultimately produce a more capable citizenry and more perfect polity and in the belief that no other approach would comport with the premise of individual dignity and choice upon which our political system rests. . . .
>
> That the air may at times seem filled with verbal cacophony is, in this sense, not a sign of weakness but of strength. We cannot lose sight of the fact that, in what otherwise might seem . . . [an] individual['s] distasteful abuse of a privilege, these fundamental societal values are truly implicated.

Many Americans may well consider other messages even more disfavored, disturbing, and feared than "hate speech"—for example, flag burning or advocating terrorism. After all, the opposition to flag burning has been so strong that it has fueled a proposed constitutional amendment to make an exception to the First Amendment to permit its punishment, and this amendment has received super-majority votes in both Houses of Congress. There has been no parallel effort concerning constitutionally protected "hate speech." Likewise, since the 9/11 terrorist attacks, laws that are aimed at checking terrorism have sailed through Congress and state legislatures. If our legal system permitted "hate speech" laws as exceptions to the viewpoint neutrality and emergency rules, we could then anticipate additional "exceptional" laws barring other unpopular expression, including speech that is viewed as unpatriotic or endangering our national security.

In 1977–78, when the ACLU defended the free speech rights of neo-Nazis to hold a demonstration in Skokie, Illinois, which had a large Jewish population, including many Holocaust survivors, many ACLU members resigned from the organization in protest. Even though they were generally stalwart free speech supporters, they maintained that they drew the line at this particular expression. Yet, as a former executive director of the National Coalition Against Censorship observed, "Everyone has his or her Skokie." All of us hold some perspectives to be especially abhorrent, disturbing, or frightening, but we vary widely as to exactly what those are. Such especially reviled ideas are as broad and diverse as the views and values that we all hold. Assuming, purely hypothetically, that our legal system could make "just one" exception to the cardinal viewpoint neutrality and emergency principles for constitutionally protected "hate speech," there would be overwhelming political pressures to make "just one more" exception, over and over again.

The Court's increasingly strict enforcement of the viewpoint neutrality principle (and its complementary emergency test) is the most effective vehicle, in practice as well as in principle, for protecting *all* controversial expression. Neither the vehemence with which officials or citizens oppose particular views, nor the widespread nature of that opposition, warrants any exception to this crucial principle. As the Supreme Court has said: "The fact that society may find speech offensive is not a sufficient reason for suppressing it. Indeed, if it is the speaker's opinion that gives offense, that . . . is a reason for according it constitutional protection."

The difficulty—indeed, impossibility—of cabining exceptions to the viewpoint neutrality and emergency principles solely for constitutionally protected "hate speech," or for some subset of such speech, is signaled by the experience in other countries with "hate speech" laws. As I recount in Chapter 4, in response to predictable political pressures, such laws have expanded in scope over time, and they have emboldened lawmakers to punish other speech expressing other disfavored views.

CHAPTER THREE

When "Hate Speech" Is Protected and When It Is Punishable

THUS FAR, I HAVE explained the contours of constitutionally protected "hate speech" under American law, consistent with the viewpoint neutrality and emergency principles. In this chapter, I describe the situations in which "hate speech" is *not* constitutionally protected and hence may be punished. Only by understanding both facets of our free speech jurisprudence can we accurately assess the potential costs and benefits of changing it by permitting "hate speech" laws.

As already noted, government may constitutionally punish "hate speech"—just as it may punish speech conveying any other message—consistent with the emergency test, when the speech directly causes specific imminent serious harm. That test is strict, and it must be as strictly enforced when the targeted expression is "hate speech" as when the speech conveys any other message. Even so, the emergency test has been satisfied by significant instances of "hate speech," including many that proponents of "hate speech" laws cite as ostensibly illustrating the need for such laws. To be sure, these advocates seek to expand our government's authority to suppress "hate speech" far beyond the situations when it may already do so. To assess the pros and cons of such expanded censorial powers, it is important to be aware of the situations in which "hate speech" already may be restricted.

"HATE SPEECH" CAN BE PUNISHED IN SEVERAL SITUATIONS

Proponents of "hate speech" laws regularly understate the extent to which American law already permits regulation of "hate speech" in particular contexts. A recent example is a 2016 op-ed by University of Utah law professor Amos Guiora, entitled "In This Age of Internet Hate, It's Time to Revisit Limits on Free Speech." His op-ed begins by citing six recent examples of what he dubs "hate speech"—but only one of his examples is in fact protected by the First Amendment. Guiora's piece offers the following examples:

> Swastikas spray-painted on the door of a Colorado elementary school and on several college campuses. A rally for the president-elect of the United States featuring a "Heil Hitler" salute. A proposed registry for Muslims . . .
>
> Benjamin Kuperman, a professor at Oberlin College, awoke to sounds of tapping outside his home to find . . . a note behind his mezuzah (a small case that contains verses from the Torah, common for Jews to place on their door frames) that stated, "Gas Jews Die." A similar scenario unfolded at Harvard University, where a professor recently received a postcard stating, "Juden raus!," a phrase introduced by the Nazis that means "Jews out."

Guiora then goes on to assert: "To some, these incidents are clear-cut examples of hate speech. To others, expressing the viewpoint of the so-called white nationalist movement is a First Amendment right that should be allowed—and celebrated—as free speech without censorship."

Guiora is indeed correct that the First Amendment bars the government from censoring expression solely because of its disfavored, disturbing, or feared viewpoint, including such a repugnant viewpoint as white nationalism. For that reason, one example he cites—but one only—would be protected under current U.S. law: the symbolic expression of the Nazi salute at the Trump rally. As I have explained, First Amendment principles correctly prevent government from censoring such political expression. These principles likewise protect all other symbolic expression that conveys controversial ideas, including other ideas about racial solidarity and superiority, such as the Black Power salute. The latter has repeatedly spurred controversy recently, including when used by supporters of the Black Lives Matter movement, in superstar Beyoncé's 2016 Super Bowl halftime show, and by a group of female African-American cadets at West Point. In all of these instances, though, the speech was constitutionally protected, and the single instance of constitutionally protected "hate speech" that Guiora cites is, similarly, insulated from government censorship.

In contrast, all of Guiora's other examples involve expression that may constitutionally be prohibited under current law. The swastikas spray-painted on school and college facilities may be punished because they constitute a crime that is independent of the message conveyed: namely, vandalism. Moreover, the two threatening notes that were attached and/or mailed to the homes of Jewish professors may constitutionally be punished because they constitute illegal threats. Finally, the elected officials' proposed registry for Muslims, far from being protected by the First Amendment, would actually violate the First Amendment, by deterring Muslims from exercising both their free speech and religious liberty rights under the Constitution.

In sum, all but one of the situations that Guiora cites as ostensibly supporting the need to "revisit limits on free speech" instead prove the opposite: that existing free speech principles permit outlawing and punishing the actions to which he (understandably) objects. And the last such situation, the Nazi salute, could not be punished without unleashing government power to punish any symbolic expression with a message that is disfavored, disturbing, or feared.

SOME CONTEXTS IN WHICH "HATE SPEECH"

MAY CONSTITUTIONALLY BE RESTRICTED

The Private Sector

Many people are surprised to learn that the First Amendment, like almost all constitutional guarantees, restricts only *government* action. Except in unusual situations, it imposes no limit on private-sector individuals or entities. Accordingly, private entities are generally free—in terms of the Constitution—to restrict "hate speech" whenever they wish to do so. A private employer, for example, is generally legally free to fire an employee who engages in on-the-job speech of which the employer disapproves. As I explained in Chapter 1, though, I urge respect for free speech principles even in contexts when the First Amendment does not mandate them, including in the private sector.

At the same time, though, I would support "hate speech" restrictions that are maximally narrow and precise in some private-sector contexts. For example, employers may forbid on-duty employees from using "hate speech" when addressing members of the public. Such a policy would further equality and antidiscrimination values and would also serve the employer's legitimate business interests. Moreover, "hate speech" in this context, especially if repeated or combined with discriminatory conduct, can violate civil rights laws that forbid discrimination by businesses that are open to the general public. Professional associations constitute another private sphere in which I would endorse bans on certain "hate speech," defined as clearly and narrowly as feasible. For example, a lawyer would violate standards of professional responsibility, and undermine our system of justice, by addressing racially insulting language to participants in courtroom proceedings.

My primary concern in this book is when *government* may regulate "hate speech" consistent with the First Amendment. What follows are several examples of that phenomenon.

Viewpoint-Neutral Regulations

Government may sometimes shield people from "hate speech" by enforcing viewpoint-neutral "time, place, and manner regulations," which impose reasonable limits on when, where, and how speech is conveyed. For example, recognizing "the sanctity of the home" as a "retreat . . . from . . . tribulations," whose "tranquility . . . and privacy" should be protected from intrusive communications, government may forbid the use of loudspeakers in residential neighborhoods at night, as long as it does so in a viewpoint-neutral manner. To pass First Amendment muster, viewpoint-neutral regulations must leave speakers "ample alternative communications channels" for conveying their messages, and the government must show that the regulations are "narrowly tailored to serve a significant government interest" and are not intended to disfavor the expression of any particular point of view. Consistent with these conditions, government may regulate "hate speech" in the same way as speech with any other message. For instance, if a public university is concerned that some signs posted in a dormitory might for some residents disturb the "tranquility" of this home, it could simply ban *all* signs in dormitories' shared residential spaces.

Special-Purpose Facilities

In certain government facilities that are designed to serve a specific purpose, the Supreme Court has held that government may impose reasonable speech restrictions to facilitate that purpose, even if those restrictions would not be constitutional in the general public sphere. Such special-purpose government facilities include government workplaces, prisons and jails, military installations, and public schools. In such settings, the government has some latitude to restrict speech, including "hate speech," if the speech directly interferes with the government's functioning. For example, consistent with the government's constitutional duty to treat all members of the public equally, government employees can be disciplined for using "hate speech" when interacting with members of the public in their official capacities.

In the public school context, where vibrant free speech fosters the school's educational mission, the Supreme Court has held that some expression by students or teachers may be restricted, but only when it "substantially" or "materially" "disrupts the educational process." Although the Court has not reviewed any case in which a public school has barred "hate speech," a number of lower courts have upheld such restrictions. For example, where schools have experienced racial violence and tensions, courts have upheld rules against student clothing displaying words or symbols that some people have deemed "hate speech," including the Confederate flag and slogans endorsing "White Power" or "Black Lives Matter." Courts should strictly enforce the substantial disruption standard to ensure that schools do not invoke it as a pretext for suppressing ideas that teachers or administrators disfavor. The Supreme Court stressed this point in its landmark 1969 ruling in *Tinker v. Des Moines School District*, which upheld students' right to wear black armbands to protest the Vietnam War. That antiwar perspective was highly controversial at the time, therefore predictably provoking anger and hurt on the part of some members of the school community, including those with close relatives who were fighting and had even been killed in Vietnam. Nonetheless, the Court held that "undifferentiated fear or apprehension of disturbance is not enough to overcome the right to freedom of expression."

Government Speech

Under the "government speech" doctrine, the government has the prerogative to choose which messages it will convey, and which it will eschew. For citizens who object to such choices, the remedy is at the ballot box. In short, although the viewpoint neutrality principle requires the government to permit citizens to express all sorts of competing messages, whether the government likes them or not, the government itself may choose to speak in its own voice without violating the First Amendment. For this reason, the First Amendment does not bar government from choosing to eliminate any official expression, including symbolic displays, that convey messages the government itself does not wish to support, such as Confederate flags or statues of Confederate leaders.

RESTRICTING "HATE SPEECH" UNDER THE EMERGENCY TEST

Consistent with the emergency principle, government may punish speech when necessary to avert serious harm that cannot be averted through non-censorial measures—notably, law enforcement and counterspeech. Accordingly, government may punish "hate speech" (or speech conveying any other message) when, in context, it directly, demonstrably, and imminently causes certain specific, objectively ascertainable serious harms. The Supreme Court has identified several kinds of situations in which speech satisfies this general emergency standard, specifying particular criteria for each. These criteria are appropriately strict, to circumscribe officials' opportunity to assert the potential harm as a pretext for suppressing speech merely because its message is disfavored, disturbing, or feared. When any speech satisfies these criteria, though—including "hate speech"—it may be restricted.

True Threats

The Supreme Court has held that government may constitutionally punish what it has labeled "true threats." True threats are limited to statements through which "the speaker means to communicate a serious expression of an intent to commit an act of unlawful violence to a particular individual or group of individuals" and, in consequence, the targeted individuals reasonably fear that violence. This standard is satisfied if the speaker has "knowledge that the communication will be viewed as" conveying such a threat. The speaker need not actually intend to commit the threatened act; this standard recognizes that the reasonable fear of the act constitutes serious harm in itself, which can have such adverse consequences as hampering the threatened person's freedoms of movement and speech.

The true threat concept considers the full context of the expression. Therefore, even such a generally threatening symbol as a burning cross, which is inextricably associated with the Ku Klux Klan's racist terrorism, is not necessarily punishable as a true threat. For example, the Supreme Court has held that the true threat standard was not satisfied when Klan members burned crosses at members-only rallies that others could not see. In different settings, though, including burning a cross on the property of an African-American family, such speech could clearly constitute a punishable true threat.

Similarly, in a range of circumstances, including in workplaces and on college campuses, the display of a noose could constitute a punishable true threat. For example, on May 1, 2017, six pairs of bananas strung in nooses were displayed on American University's campus in Washington, D.C. under circumstances in which they conveyed a true threat to student Taylor Dumpson, who on that day became the university's first African-American student body president. The conclusion that these displays meant to convey a threat to harm Ms. Dumpson was made clear by messages that were written on them, including: "AKA FREE," referring to the predominantly African-American sorority Alpha Kappa Alpha, of which Ms. Dumpson was a member; and "HARAMBE BAIT," the name of the Cincinnati Zoo gorilla that was killed in 2016 after a child had fallen into its enclosure.

On the other hand, the Supreme Court has recognized that even explicitly threatening words may not rise to the level of a punishable true threat when one considers the full factual context. In *Watts v. United States*, for example, the Court held that threatening language in a public debate was mere hyperbolic rhetoric that would not instill reasonable fear of an actual attack. At a Washington, D.C. rally protesting police brutality, Robert Watts, an 18-year-old African-American man, referring to then-President Lyndon Baines Johnson, made the following statement: "I have already received my draft classification as 1-A. . . . If they ever make me carry a rifle the first man I want to get in my sights is L.B.J. They are not going to make me kill my black brothers." Watts was convicted of threatening the president. However, characterizing Watts's statement as "political hyperbole," the Supreme Court reversed his conviction, explaining that "[t]he language used in the political arena . . . is often vituperative, abusive and inexact." The Court's ruling protects today's young people who are following in Robert Watts's footsteps, also condemning police abuse and racial discrimination with sometimes very strong language.

Punishable Incitement

> "Our history illustrates that unless very narrowly constrained, the power to restrict the advocacy of violence is an invitation to punish political dissent. A. Mitchell Palmer, J. Edgar Hoover, and Joseph McCarthy all used the advocacy of violence as a justification to punish people who associated with Communists, socialists, or civil rights groups."
>
> —David Cole, ACLU Legal Director

In everyday speech, we use the term "incitement" loosely to describe expression that might induce those to whom it is communicated to commit a violent or otherwise illegal act. In the landmark 1969 case of *Brandenburg v. Ohio*, the Supreme Court unanimously held that speech constitutes constitutionally punishable incitement only if the speaker intentionally incites imminent violent or otherwise illegal conduct that is likely to occur immediately. The Court held that the First Amendment therefore protected the following statements that a Ku Klux Klan leader made at a rally of his followers: "Personally, I believe the [N-word] should be returned to Africa, the Jew returned to Israel. . . . We're not a revengent [*sic*] organization, but if our President, our Congress, our Supreme Court, continues to suppress the white, Caucasian race, it's possible that there might have to be some revengeance [*sic*] taken."

Enforcing this narrow concept of punishable incitement, thirteen years later the Court held in *Claiborne Hardware v. NAACP* that NAACP officials had a First Amendment right to threaten violent reprisals against people who violated an NAACP-organized boycott of white merchants who allegedly had engaged in racial discrimination. NAACP field organizer Charles Evers warned boycott violators: "If we catch any of you going in any of them racist stores, we're gonna break your damn neck." Although several acts of violence were subsequently committed against African Americans who patronized white merchants, the Court held that Evers's words did not constitute punishable incitement because the violent acts occurred weeks or months later, so the critical "imminency" standard was not satisfied. The Court explained that we must tolerate such speech because "strong and effective extemporaneous rhetoric cannot be nicely channeled in purely dulcet phrases. An advocate must be free to stimulate his audience with . . . emotional appeals."

This is not to say that there are no circumstances in which government may punish "hate speech" under the strict incitement standard. An example is afforded by a 1993 Supreme Court case involving a group of young African-American men who were discussing a scene from the motion picture *Mississippi Burning*, which is about the 1960s civil rights movement. The scene showed a white man beating up a young black boy who was praying. Enraged by this scene, one of the African-American men, Todd Mitchell, asked the others, "Do you all feel hyped up to move on some white people?" Shortly thereafter, a white boy approached the group on the opposite side of the street where they were standing. As the boy walked by, Mitchell said to his companions: "You all want to fuck somebody up? There goes a white boy; go get him." Mitchell counted to three and pointed in the boy's direction. The group ran toward the boy and beat him severely. Although the Supreme Court upheld the conviction on a different rationale, Mitchell's speech clearly satisfied the punishable incitement standard.

Fighting Words

"Fighting words" constitute a type of punishable incitement: when speakers intentionally incite imminent violence against themselves (in contrast with third parties), which is likely to happen immediately. In the fighting words situation the speaker hurls insulting language directly at another person, intending to instigate that person's imminent violent reaction against the speaker himself/herself, and that violence is likely to occur immediately. The Supreme Court upheld a fighting words conviction in the 1942 case of *Chaplinsky v. New Hampshire.* This was decades before the Court began to meaningfully protect freedom of speech by strictly enforcing the viewpoint neutrality and emergency principles. It was also before the Court narrowed the fighting words doctrine to make it consistent with the general concept of punishable incitement. Since *Chaplinsky,* the Court has overturned every single fighting words conviction that it has reviewed. Nonetheless, certain "hate speech" could satisfy even the current strict standard. Imagine, for example, a member of the Ku Klux Klan personally insulting a Black Lives Matter activist with racist epithets, or vice versa. Such individually targeted, deliberately provocative "hate speech" presumably could be punished under the fighting words doctrine.

Harassment

Consistent with the First Amendment, the government may punish specific "hate speech" in certain circumstances as sanctionable harassment. For example, the government may punish expression that directly targets an individual or small group of individuals in a manner that, under all the facts and circumstances, unduly harries or intrudes upon the targeted individuals' freedom or privacy. A classic example would be repeated unwanted telephone calls in the middle of the night, thus disturbing the targeted individual's privacy and rest. Many "hate speech" incidents that are cited as purportedly demonstrating the need for new "hate speech" laws would already be punishable as targeted harassment. One prominent example was stressed by Professor Charles Lawrence in his influential law review article advocating campus "hate speech" codes: a group of white male students at Stanford University followed a female African-American student across campus, shouting, "I've never tried a [N-word] before."

Another variant of this theme is "hostile environment" harassment, which typically arises in a workplace. The Supreme Court has ruled that persistent harassment may be punished if it is sufficiently "severe or pervasive to alter the conditions of [the victim's] employment and create an abusive working environment." This hostile environment harassment concept has been applied to educational contexts as well. In contrast with targeted harassment, the expression need not be directed at an individual or small group of individuals; it may include expression that is addressed generally to large groups, such as a lecture. Also in contrast with targeted harassment, the concern here is specifically with the hateful, discriminatory message. For these reasons, hostile environment harassment raises especially serious free speech concerns. Therefore, the Supreme Court has stressed that offensive expression alone usually will not give rise to a claim of hostile environment harassment, and that it could do so only if the expression were "so severe, pervasive, and objectively offensive, that it effectively bars the victim's access" to the workplace or "to an educational opportunity or benefit." If "hate speech" (or any other speech) satisfied these demanding standards, it could be restricted. The federal Equal Employment Opportunity Commission (EEOC) recently settled a case in which it charged that a company's African-American employees had been subjected to a racially hostile work environment due to multiple incidents of "hate speech": a noose was displayed at the worksite; derogatory racial language was used by a direct supervisor and a manager of these employees, including references to the Ku Klux Klan; and the employees had been targeted with racial insults.

Facilitating Criminal Conduct

Government may punish expression that intentionally provides essential information for carrying out illegal acts because it inflicts an independent harm, thus diminishing concern that government is seeking to suppress unpopular ideas. The most notorious example of "hate speech" that has been punished for this reason is the virulent anti-Tutsi radio propaganda that Rwandan radio station RTLM broadcast during the 1994 genocide of the Tutsis by the Hutus. Some such expression constituted punishable incitement, and some of it went beyond incitement to provide information that facilitated the genocidal murders. Article 19, the international free speech organization, described RTLM's role as actually "organis[ing]" genocide, "notably by identifying targets . . . [and] refuges where potential victims were hiding."

Bias Crimes

Some "hate speech" may be punished indirectly, when it constitutes evidence of a bias crime. For example, in the *Mississippi Burning* case that I described above, the Court held that the government could treat the African-American youths' assault on the white boy as a bias crime, supporting that conclusion with the hateful, discriminatory, inciting words that the defendant had uttered immediately before the assault.

CONSTITUTIONALLY PROTECTED "HATE SPEECH"

When we synthesize the various situations in which "hate speech" may be constrained, they provide the following parameters for when government may and may not regulate such speech in the general public sphere: *Government may not regulate "hate speech" solely because its message is disfavored, disturbing, or feared. But government may restrict "hate speech" when it directly, demonstrably, and imminently causes certain specific, objectively ascertainable serious harms.*

Readers might well ask: "Since constitutionally protected 'hate speech' is only a subset of all 'hate speech,' then wouldn't it be no big deal to censor it too, along with the 'hate speech' that is already punishable?" The answer is a resounding *"No!"* for two reasons.

First, although the government may restrict instances of "hate speech" in a range of contexts, the domain of constitutionally protected "hate speech" is virtually infinite; it encompasses speech discussing limitless subjects and conveying countless perspectives, including perspectives on the most urgent public policy issues of the day. Second, "hate speech" laws would immeasurably harm freedom of speech by departing from the viewpoint neutrality and emergency tests, which govern the situations in which our law now permits regulation of "hate speech."

The adverse impact of empowering government to suppress "hate speech" beyond the bounds marked by the viewpoint neutrality and emergency principles was well stated by German professor Winfried Brugger. Discussing his country's "hate speech" laws, he wrote: "A distant and generalized threat to the public peace and to . . . dignity . . . suffices for legal sanctions irrespective of whether and when such danger would actually manifest itself. . . . [G]overnment's task in this area [is] control of the political climate ('Klimakontrolle')."

In the United States, we have opposed such government control of ideas feared to be vaguely dangerous, because it would produce a political climate that is too chilly for vibrant discourse.

Let me cite just two examples of the kinds of statements that have garnered official sanction under Germany's "hate speech" laws, with their goal of political climate control: a retired woman was punished for holding a sign at a political rally comparing the threat that Muslims and Turks now pose to Europe to the seventeenth-century Ottoman Empire invasion of Europe; and German courts imposed a three-month prison sentence on a historian for statements he made about Nazi history in a private letter he sent to another historian. Whether we agree or disagree with the statements at issue, most Americans would not want "Big Brother" again to have the power to punish such statements, which was wielded in the past to suppress dissent and debate.

CHAPTER FOUR

Because of Their Intractable Vagueness and Overbreadth, "Hate Speech" Laws Undermine Free Speech and Equality

"I know it when I see it."

—Supreme Court Justice Potter Stewart

"A vague law impermissibly delegates basic policy matters to policemen, judges, and juries for resolution on an *ad hoc* and subjective basis, with the attendant dangers of arbitrary and discriminatory application."

—Supreme Court, *Grayned v. City of Rockford* (1972)

THE SUPREME COURT has held that any law is "unduly vague," and hence unconstitutional, when people "of common intelligence must necessarily guess at its meaning." This violates tenets of "due process" or fairness, as well as equality, because such a law is inherently susceptible to arbitrary and discriminatory enforcement. Moreover, when an unduly vague law regulates speech in particular, the law also violates the First Amendment because it inevitably deters people from engaging in constitutionally protected speech for fear that they might run afoul of the law. The Supreme Court has therefore enforced the "void for vagueness" doctrine with special strictness in the context of laws that regulate speech.

As I have already explained, "hate speech" laws violate the cardinal viewpoint neutrality and emergency principles, which are designed to constrain official discretion to punish speech, and in particular to prevent government officials from restricting the expression of particular ideas because they view the ideas as disfavored, disturbing, or vaguely dangerous. Unmoored from these critical limits, "hate speech" laws invariably turn on inherently subjective, elastic words and concepts, including "hate." Such laws therefore endow enforcing authorities with largely unfettered discretion to choose which ideas and speakers to single out for investigation and punishment. They inevitably exercise this discretion in accord with their own self-interest or their personal judgments about which speech is or is not worthy of protection.

For two reasons, this discretionary enforcement is inimical to both free speech and equality. First, the discretion predictably will be wielded in a way that disfavors disempowered people and unpopular ideas. Second, the law will have a significant chilling effect, deterring people from expressing points of view that might be subject to investigation or punishment. "Hate speech" laws likely induce an especially frigid chill because most people do not want even to be accused of engaging in such expression, regardless of how important they might consider the ideas at stake.

Another closely related problem that "hate speech" laws pose is what lawyers term "substantial overbreadth": "hate speech" laws tend to be written in such capacious language that they extend to speech that even the laws' proponents do not seek to punish. Although these laws could be relatively confined in scope, thus reducing the overbreadth problem, the undue vagueness problems appear to be inescapable.

Even if we were to put aside the viewpoint neutrality and emergency principles—which we should *not* do—"hate speech" laws would still undermine free speech and equality because of their intrinsic vagueness and overbreadth. Because of these problems, as I demonstrate in this chapter, "hate speech" laws have regularly been enforced in ways that are inconsistent with and even undermine their purposes.

THE SPECIAL PROBLEMS OF AMBIGUITY
IN "HATE SPEECH" LAWS

Given the limits of language, no statutory wording can eliminate all ambiguities. First Amendment law therefore recognizes that some degree of vagueness and overbreadth is unavoidable, as signaled by the fact that First Amendment doctrine bars only statutory language that is "unduly" vague or "substantially" overbroad. But when government regulates political speech, such as "hate speech," the Court enforces these requirements more strictly. To afford such highly valued speech the "breathing space" it needs "to survive," "government may regulate . . . only with narrow specificity."

In cases involving other forms of controversial political speech the Court has consistently struck down statutory terms that are frequently contained in "hate speech" laws—for example, "contemptuous," "insulting," "abusive," and "outrageous." In a 1988 case, for example, the Court invalidated a statute that outlawed certain speech that undermined the "dignity" of foreign embassy personnel. Some proponents of "hate speech" laws seek to justify them as protecting the "dignity" of disparaged people. In the embassy case, though, the Court made clear that the censorial law at issue, like "hate speech" laws, "operates at the core of the First Amendment by prohibiting . . . classically political speech." It then explained:

> [I]n public debate our . . . citizens must tolerate insulting, and even outrageous, speech in order to provide adequate "breathing space" to the freedoms protected by the First Amendment. A "dignity" standard, like the "outrageousness" standard that we rejected in [an earlier case], is so inherently subjective that it would be inconsistent with "our longstanding refusal to [punish speech] because [it] may have an adverse emotional impact on the audience."

Similarly, the "inherently subjective" standards typically found in "hate speech" laws effectively license government to punish speech solely because its disfavored ideas are thought to have a disturbing or "adverse emotional impact on the audience."

The inescapable fact is that the very subject matter of "hate speech" laws—a disfavored, disturbing, and feared emotion—is insusceptible to precise, narrow definition. In part for that reason, every campus "hate speech" code that courts have reviewed has been struck down on vagueness or overbreadth grounds, including codes that were drafted by or with the assistance of faculty First Amendment experts, who presumably selected optimally precise, narrow language. Moreover, as I show in Chapter 5, the multiple phrasing options that have been proposed for or adopted in "hate speech" laws worldwide reveal apparently insurmountable vagueness and overbreadth problems.

A "HATE SPEECH" LAW THAT IS RELATIVELY NARROW OR
PRECISE WILL RAISE OTHER FIRST AMENDMENT PROBLEMS

Let us assume, solely for the sake of argument, that one could draft a law delineating a relatively narrow subset of constitutionally protected "hate speech," thus reducing the overbreadth problems. That still would not solve the insurmountable vagueness problems. Consider, for example, law professor Mari Matsuda's influential proposal to outlaw only messages "of racial inferiority . . . directed against a historically oppressed group," which are "persecutorial, hateful, and degrading." This proposed "hate speech" law is relatively narrow, incorporating several limits on the outlawed speech, in terms of both its message and its targets. Yet at least some of the limiting factors themselves are irreducibly vague.

Consider the following illustration Matsuda provides of the distinction she attempts to draw between protected and punishable "hate speech": an expression of "[a] belief in intellectual differences between the races . . . is not subject to sanctions unless it is coupled with an element of hatred or persecution." Now consider whether Professor Charles Murray's controversial writings on this topic would satisfy Matsuda's standard. As recent campus protests against him have shown, many critics of his writings assert that they do reflect "hatred or persecution," but other critics of his views would reject that characterization. Indeed, Matsuda recognizes the vagueness problems with her standard and discusses multiple examples of speech that, she acknowledges, arguably could either satisfy or not satisfy her definition. In short, people "of ordinary intelligence must guess at [the] meaning" of her proposed law, rendering it unacceptably vague.

In addition to not solving the vagueness problem, narrowing the scope of a "hate speech" law ironically increases other First Amendment problems. First, the less constitutionally protected "hate speech" a law suppresses, and the more such speech it leaves protected, the less effective the law is in reducing the harms that are said to justify it. In weighing whether a speech-suppressive law is justified, courts—consistent with common logic—assess how effectively it promotes its goals. Accordingly, courts will strike down a law that curtails speech without meaningfully redressing the problem that the targeted speech allegedly causes; in such a situation, the law's free speech costs are not sufficiently offset by its purported benefits.

A narrower law also presents special dangers of viewpoint discrimination. As the Supreme Court has explained, if a law is "under-inclusive when judged against its asserted justification," this "raises . . . doubts about whether the government is in fact pursuing the interest it invokes, rather than disfavoring a particular speaker or viewpoint." In a 1991 case, for example, the Supreme Court struck down a "hate speech" law that had been enacted in St. Paul, Minnesota, in order to foster intergroup harmony, because it selectively outlawed only "abusive invective" that was based on "race, color, creed, religion or gender." The Court observed that St. Paul thus permitted speakers to use "abusive invective, no matter how vicious or severe," to "express hostility" on any other basis, including "political affiliation, union membership, or homosexuality," concluding that "the First Amendment does not permit St. Paul to impose special prohibitions on those speakers who express views on disfavored subjects." In this situation, the law is not unconstitutionally overbroad, but rather, unconstitutionally selective or underinclusive. In effect, such a law embodies viewpoint discrimination, contravening the viewpoint neutrality principle.

The only way to constrain the unfettered discretion that unduly vague "hate speech" laws vest in government officials would be to replace open-textured, malleable criteria with specific, inflexible ones. To the best of my knowledge, no proponent of "hate speech" laws endorses such an approach, in part because it causes more problems than it solves. The major advocates of these laws in the United States maintain that any "hate speech" must be assessed contextually, and not inflexibly punished based solely on its language. They reach this conclusion about even such a universally reviled racist slur as the "N-word," suggesting that it should be judged in light of all the facts and circumstances in which it is uttered. The resulting undue vagueness problem would afflict even a "hate speech" law that was relatively narrow in scope.

Readers may well now be asking: How can the government avoid all of the First Amendment problems I have just outlined? How can a law avoid both the rock of undue vagueness and the hard place of undue rigidity? How can it avoid both the frying pan of substantial overbreadth and the fire of undue narrowness? The answer lies in the speech-protective emergency standard. As I have explained in earlier chapters, Justices Oliver Wendell Holmes and Louis Brandeis forged this test in the early twentieth century as an alternative to the unduly vague and overbroad bad tendency test that the Court's majority was then employing to the great detriment of liberty, equality, and democracy. The emergency test also avoids undue rigidity because it is contextual, not focusing on words alone but also taking into account all pertinent facts and circumstances. Finally, by its very terms the emergency test targets all speech that directly causes specific imminent serious harm, so it is effective in checking such harm; indeed, the emergency test has been aptly described as "effects-based, not viewpoint-based."

ILLUSTRATIONS OF THESE INTRACTABLE DRAFTING PROBLEMS

Authorities who have enforced "hate speech" laws have struggled to draw distinctions between punishable and protected speech. Consider, for example, the Canadian Supreme Court's explications of the term "hatred" in that nation's laws punishing speech "that is likely to expose" people to "hatred or contempt": "unusually strong and deep-felt emotions of detestation, calumny and vilification"; and "enmity and extreme ill-will . . . which goes beyond mere disdain or dislike." If you were a juror, would you be able to distinguish between speech that conveys "disdain," which is not punishable, and speech that conveys "detestation" or "vilification," which is? And if you were voicing your own strongly negative views about some person or group, how secure would you feel that officials would consider your words to communicate protected "disdain" rather than punishable "enmity" or "extreme ill-will"?

Let me cite one recent ironic illustration of the endemic vagueness and overbreadth problems that bedevil all "hate speech" laws. It comes from the December 2015 report by the European Commission against Racism and Intolerance (ECRI), an expert body that monitors implementation of European "hate speech" laws. Like other expert agencies, ECRI has concluded that European "hate speech" laws can be enforced "to silence minorities and to suppress criticism, political opposition and religious beliefs." Accordingly, this ECRI report recommended that European governments should amend their laws' definitions of illegal "hate speech" "to ensure that they are clearly and precisely worded." Ironically, though, the report itself offered a definition that was hardly "clearly and precisely worded," thus underscoring the elusiveness of this goal. Here is the report's proposed definition of illegal "hate speech":

> [Hate speech] excludes any form of expression . . . that merely offends, hurts or distresses. . . . Nonetheless, . . . [prohibited] incitement to hatred can result from insulting [or] holding up to ridicule . . . specific groups . . . where such forms of expression are exercised in an irresponsible manner—which might entail being unnecessarily offensive . . . or using vexatious or humiliating language.

This purportedly clarifying definition obviously raises more questions than it answers, including how to draw the line between expression that "merely offends," which is protected, and expression that is "unnecessarily offensive," which is punishable.

The impossibility of writing a sufficiently clear, narrow "hate speech" law is indicated by reports by the major international human rights organizations Amnesty International and Human Rights Watch. As one commentator has noted, these groups' reports about various countries' hate speech laws "criticize the [laws'] imprecise, ill-defined, broad and vague nature" and "demand more 'certainty'" but "offer no solutions," thus "reveal[ing] [the organizations'] inability . . . to give clear recommendations" for acceptable language.

Let me now cite an example of these insoluble drafting problems from the United States. As I have pointed out, the campus "hate speech" codes that were adopted, starting in the late 1980s, consistently have been struck down when challenged in court, because their language is unduly vague and overbroad. Typical is the University of Michigan's "hate speech" code, which was one of the first to be adopted, and which led to the first judicial decision about these unavoidable First Amendment flaws. Federal judge Avern Cohn found that the following key terms, describing the punishable speech, were unduly vague: "stigmatize," "victimize," and "threats to" or "interfering with an individual's academic efforts."

During the oral argument, when Judge Cohn asked the university's attorney how he would distinguish the proscribed speech from other offensive speech, which the attorney conceded was protected, the attorney answered, "Very carefully." Welcome as this answer is in its candor and humor, the point at issue is no laughing matter. When even the university's legal counsel cannot explain the distinction between protected and punishable speech, all members of the campus community face enforcement that is unpredictable and inconsistent at best, and arbitrary, capricious, and discriminatory at worst.

As I noted above, the Canadian Supreme Court attempted to rein in officials' discretion in enforcing Canadian "hate speech" laws by defining the key statutory terms "hatred or contempt." Nonetheless, Canadian officials, including judges, have continued to disagree about whether particular speech does or does not satisfy these definitions. Consider, for example, a case in which a man was charged under a Canadian "hate speech" law for distributing four flyers expressing his opposition to homosexuality based on his Christian beliefs. The administrative tribunal that first heard the case ruled that all of the flyers violated the law. The trial-level court that reviewed this decision affirmed it, but the intermediate appellate court reversed as to all four flyers, concluding that none of them constituted illegal "hate speech." Finally, Canada's Supreme Court held that two of the flyers did constitute illegal "hate speech," but that two did not. In sum, with respect to the same set of communications, the four expert judicial bodies arrived at a total of three different conclusions as to which of them, if any, constituted punishable "hate speech."

Having read many administrative and judicial rulings from countries all over the world enforcing their variously worded "hate speech" laws, I have been struck by how typical this Canadian case is. Over and over, different decision-makers in the same country disagree about whether particular expression does or does not fall afoul of the pertinent "hate speech" laws.

The confounding problem of deciding what should count as "hate speech" was also illustrated by a situation at Harvard University, when some students hung Confederate flags from their dormitory windows, which prompted other students to protest by hanging swastikas from their dormitory windows. Of course, the swastika is deeply identified with Hitler's anti-Semitic and other egregiously hateful ideas, not to mention genocide. However, the Harvard students who hung the swastika were trying to convey the opposite message, condemning the racism that the Confederate flag connoted to them by equating it with the swastika. So should these swastika displays count as "hate speech"—or as *anti-*"hate speech"?

Then, in a separate protest against the discriminatory message that the Confederate flags conveyed to them, other Harvard students engaged in another form of counterspeech: they publicly burned a Confederate flag. To the many Americans who revere the Confederate flag as a symbol of their Southern heritage and a tribute to their ancestors who were killed in the Civil War, burning this cherished symbol constitutes "hate speech." Yet the students who set the fire sincerely believed that they were engaging in anti–"hate speech."

The topic of flag burning provides yet another illustration of the fact that one person's "hate speech" is another's anti–"hate speech." In 2015, student government leaders at the University of California, Irvine voted to ban the display of the American flag, stating that it "has been flown in instances of colonialism and imperialism, and can be interpreted as hate speech." In stark contrast, many Americans hold "Old Glory" to be so sacrosanct that they consider burning or otherwise "desecrating" it to constitute "hate speech."

ONE PERSON'S "HATE SPEECH" IS ANOTHER'S CHERISHED
SPEECH: THE PROBLEM OF HATE AND RELIGION

"[O]ne [person]'s vulgarity is another's lyric."
—Supreme Court Justice John Marshall Harlan

Given the irreducible subjectivity in assessing whether particular speech satisfies the unavoidably vague standards in "hate speech" laws, it is not surprising that one person's hated speech, conveying ideas that s/he considers hateful, is another person's cherished speech, conveying ideas that s/he considers valuable, and in some cases even loving. Here I will cite several more illustrations of this conundrum, drawn specifically from the recurring situations in which certain religious views are assailed as "hate speech" against LGBT individuals, while critiques of those religious views are attacked as anti-religious "hate speech."

Tyler Harper, a California high school student who is an evangelical Christian, wore to school a T-shirt citing a Bible verse that reflected one of his religious beliefs: "Homosexuality is Shameful, Romans 1:27." Many Christians believe that only by accepting Christian tenets, including this one, can their fellow human beings secure eternal salvation and avoid eternal damnation. With those beliefs, couldn't it be seen as compassionate and caring—indeed, loving—to proselytize? As many Christians say, they "hate the sin, but love the sinner."

In 2015, the European Union (EU) Commissioner who spearheaded new EU restrictions on "illegal online hate speech" indicated that the religious beliefs that Harper expressed should be condemned as "hate speech" under EU law. Commissioner Vera Jourova stated: "[A] narrative undermining LGBTI [lesbian, gay, bisexual, transgender, and/or intersex] rights is quietly spreading, often disguised as so-called religious principles. This is unacceptable. . . . [W]e must fight all hate speech." Jourova thereby insinuated that those who cite religious bases for opposing homosexuality are actually lying, and that they are instead animated by "hate." Ironically, this charge plausibly could be viewed as "hate speech" against religious believers. In the very same pronouncement in which she made this charge, Jourova endorsed the EU's broad concept of "hate speech," which includes expression that "incite[s] to . . . hatred directed against . . . persons . . . defined by . . . religion."

ENDANGERING MINORITY VIEWS AND SPEAKERS

"Here is the ultimate contradiction in the argument for state suppression of speech in the name of equality: it demands protection of disadvantaged minorities' interests, but in a democracy, the state acts in the name of the majority, not the minority. Why would disadvantaged minorities trust representatives of the majority to decide whose speech should be censored?"

—David Cole, ACLU legal director

Just as free speech always has been the strongest weapon to advance reform movements, including equal rights causes, censorship always has been the strongest weapon to thwart them. That general pattern applies to "hate speech" laws, even though they are adopted to advance equality. The explanation for this pattern lies in the very analysis of those who advocate for "hate speech" laws. They contend that racial minorities, women, and other groups continue to face discrimination. Precisely because I share this concern, I disagree with their prescribed solution of censorship. Given the pervasiveness of individual and institutional bias, the government is likely to enforce "hate speech" laws, as it has other laws, to the disadvantage of disempowered and marginalized groups.

Indeed, laws censoring "hate speech" have predictably been enforced against those who lack political power, including government critics and members of the very minority groups these laws are intended to protect. This concern has been raised repeatedly by international human rights organizations. For example, the most recent report by ECRI observed that, although "the duty under international law to criminalise certain forms of hate speech . . . was established to protect members of vulnerable groups," members of these groups "may have been disproportionately the subject of prosecutions" under European "hate speech" laws. Similarly, the

UN Human Rights Committee has expressed concern that "hate speech" laws can "be interpreted and enforced in an excessively broad manner, thereby targeting . . . human rights defenders [who are] promoting the elimination of racial discrimination."

This problem has been flagged even by the Committee on the Elimination of Racial Discrimination, which enforces the International Convention on the Elimination of All Forms of Racial Discrimination (CERD). This is noteworthy because CERD strongly endorses "hate speech" laws, requiring signatory countries to enact them. Thus, it is especially telling that, in light of actual experience under these laws, CERD's enforcing committee in 2013 expressed "concern that broad or vague restrictions on [hate] speech have been used to the detriment of groups protected by" CERD, and emphasized that "measures to . . . combat racist speech should not be used as a pretext to curtail expressions of protest at injustice, social discontent or opposition."

In the early 1990s, in response to then-new arguments that the United States should enact "hate speech" laws in order to promote equality, including on campus, two major international human rights organizations issued reports about how such laws operated in other countries, and both concluded that such laws too often suppressed minority views and speakers. The first report was based on an international conference in 1991 organized by the international free speech organization Article 19, which is named after the free speech guarantee in the Universal Declaration of Human Rights. That conference brought together human rights activists, lawyers, and scholars from fifteen countries to compare notes on the actual impact of "hate speech" laws in their respective countries. As Sandra Coliver, who was then Article 19's legal director, observed:

> Laws which restrict hate speech have been flagrantly abused by the authorities. Thus, the laws in Sri Lanka and South Africa

[which was then under the apartheid regime] have been used almost exclusively against the oppressed and politically weakest communities. In Eastern Europe and the former Soviet Union these laws were vehicles for the persecution of critics who were often also victims of state-tolerated or sponsored anti-Semitism. Selective or lax enforcement by the authorities, including in the United Kingdom, Israel and the former Soviet Union, allows governments to compromise the right of dissent and inevitably leads to feelings of alienation among minority groups.

Similarly, in 1992, Human Rights Watch issued a report concluding that laws that penalize hate speech are "subject to abuse by the dominant racial or ethnic group." Indeed, it observed that "[s]ome of the most stringent 'hate speech' laws . . . have long been in force in South Africa, where [under the apartheid regime] they have been used almost exclusively against the black majority." A quarter-century later, Human Rights Watch reached a similar conclusion in its 2016 report on the enforcement of "hate speech" laws in India, noting that they "are used to stifle political dissent, harass journalists, restrict activities by nongovernmental organizations, arbitrarily block Internet sites or take down content, and target religious minorities and marginalized communities, such as Dalits."

TARGETING DISSENT

"Hate speech" laws often have been used to suppress dissenting political views. In 2015, Agnès Callamard, Director of Columbia Global Freedom of Expression, observed that European "hate speech" laws often have been used to "criminalise . . . political dissent." For example, as journalist Glenn Greenwald wrote in 2017, "Cases in Turkey are common where citizens have been prosecuted under hate speech laws for criticizing government officials or the military." He also maintained that "In the UK, 'hate speech' has come to include . . . virulent criticism of UK soldiers fighting in war," citing a 2012 case of a Muslim British teenager, Azhar Ahmed, who was arrested for his strongly worded Facebook post deploring British soldiers' killing of Afghan civilians.

To further illustrate the phenomenon of "hate speech" laws being used to suppress dissenting, unpopular political views, I will cite just a few additional recent examples.

In 2017, South Africa's governing ANC party supported a new "hate speech" law to substantially expand the scope of South Africa's prior "hate speech" law, including by imposing prison sentences of up to three years for a first offense. As examples of speech that should be prosecuted under the new legislation, the ANC cited tweets by Helen Zille, the former head of the main opposition party and current premier of the Western Cape Province, in which she maintained that colonialism was not "only negative," citing as examples of its positive effect "our independent judiciary, transport infrastructure, [and] piped water." As one commentator noted: "[S]he is a politician in the official opposition and the governing party is proposing to place her in jail because of something she said. . . . [T]he proposed law . . . can be used for political persecution."

In 2017, members of German chancellor Angela Merkel's ruling coalition called for legislation imposing massive fines on social media (€50 million for the company and €5 million for its chief representative in Germany) for not promptly deleting "hate speech" on their platforms. A news story observed: "Among Germany's political establishment, there is concern that . . . racist content on social media could influence public opinion in this year's election campaign." In short, the government's proposed "hate speech" legislation could potentially be enforced to undermine political opposition.

In 2017, a Kyrgyzstan regional court affirmed a conviction and life sentence in prison for the crime of incitement of interethnic hatred. The defendant, Azimjan Askarov, is a journalist and human rights activist. An investigation by the Committee to Protect Journalists concluded that Askarov's conviction was in retaliation for his years of reporting about law enforcement corruption and human rights abuses.

In 2017, a court in Azerbaijan sentenced Faiq Amarli, the financial director of the daily national newspaper *Azadliq*, to more than three years in prison for "inciting religious hatred." This charge apparently arose from Amarli's possession of books about the teachings of Fetullah Gülen, the Turkish religious leader who is exiled in the United States. *Azadliq* is a business-focused newspaper, similar to the *Wall Street Journal*. Noting the economic ties between Azerbaijan and Turkey, the European Centre for Press and Media Freedom (ECPMF) decried Amarli's imprisonment as "one more step towards silencing the media and establishing a totalitarian regime" in Azerbaijan.

In 2015, a Singaporean court sentenced 16-year-old Amos Yee to four weeks of imprisonment for "wounding religious feelings" when he released a YouTube rant against Singapore's first prime minister, Lee Kuan Yew, shortly after Lee's death, which also included "swipes at Christianity." Shelley Thio, a Singaporean human rights activist, said that the "hate speech" charge was "politically motivated because of" Yee's criticism of "the revered elder statesman."

A 2015 study of the "hate speech" laws in Kenya and Rwanda concluded that officials have been invoking these laws in both countries "to suppress . . . legitimate speech and dissent" by "the opposition, media representatives, civil society actors, and the general public." A particularly ironic finding was that "[i]n Rwanda, hate speech legislation has [been] interpreted to bar even comments on the deficiencies of the hate speech laws themselves."

In Indonesia in 2012, Alexander Aan was sentenced to two and a half years of imprisonment and a fine of 100 million rupiah (US $10,600) for religious "hate speech" because some people construed his posts on an atheist Facebook forum as insulting to Islam.

In 2001, Britain prosecuted a longtime antinuclear activist because she had dragged an American flag on the ground during a demonstration against the controversial "Son of Star Wars" missile defense system at an American military base in England. The prosecution charged that this action was motived by "racist hatred" of the American people.

TARGETING MINORITY GROUPS

The greatest irony is when "hate speech" laws, which are designed to protect disempowered minority groups, are disproportionately used to suppress speech by or on behalf of these very groups. Because these groups lack political power, such enforcement patterns are predictable and all too common. The 2016 Human Rights Watch report about India's "hate speech" laws concluded, for example, that "too often the authorities . . . misuse" these laws "to silence . . . minority voices." In 2010, Amnesty International and Reporters Without Borders complained that in Kyrgyzstan a prominent journalist who is a member of the Uzbek minority, and the Uzbek newspaper he edited, were baselessly charged with "inciting ethnic hatred" due to their reporting on conflicts between Uzbeks and the majority Kyrgyz.

The problem of "hate speech" laws being enforced against vulnerable minority groups also occurs in more established democratic governments, including in Western Europe. As noted above, the 2015 ECRI report concluded that European "hate speech prohibitions may have been disproportionately or unjustifiably used against those whom they are intended to protect." Although the 1965 British "hate speech" law was passed to quell growing racism against minority groups, the first person convicted under it was a black man who cursed a white police officer. Throughout the 1960s and 1970s, leaders of the Black Liberation Movement in Britain were regularly prosecuted under this law. In 1968, for instance, one such leader was sentenced to a year in prison for a speech decrying the discrimination to which white people had subjected him, describing them as "vicious and nasty people." Perhaps the ultimate irony was that this law, which was intended to restrain the neo-Nazi National Front, has barred expression by the Anti-Nazi League.

Even closer to home, Canadian "hate speech" laws also have been enforced to suppress expression of minority speakers and views. In one of their first enforcement actions under these laws, Canadian Customs seized 1,500 copies of a book that various Canadian universities had tried to import from the United States. What was this dangerous racist, sexist book? None other than *Black Looks: Race and Representation*, by the African-American feminist scholar, bell hooks, who was then a professor at Oberlin College. Nor was this incident an aberration; other such perverse—but predictable—applications of Canada's "hate speech" legislation were cited by the dissenting opinion in the Canadian Supreme Court decision that narrowly upheld the law, by a closely split vote, under Canada's counterpart of the First Amendment. The dissent noted:

> Although [the law] is of relatively recent origin, it has provoked many questionable actions on the part of the authorities. . . . Intemperate statements about identifiable groups, particularly if they represent an unpopular viewpoint, may attract state involvement or calls for police action. Novels such as Leon Uris' pro-Zionist novel *The Haj*, face calls for banning. Other works,

such as Salman Rushdie's *Satanic Verses*, are stopped at the border. . . . Films may be temporarily kept out, as happened to a film entitled *Nelson Mandela*. . . . Arrests are even made for distributing pamphlets containing the words "Yankee Go Home."

Alan Borovoy, General Counsel of the Canadian Civil Liberties Association, listed even more examples of Canada's enforcement of its "hate speech" laws "against a wide variety of [speakers] who don't bear the slightest resemblance to the kind of hatemongers that were originally envisioned: . . . French-Canadian nationalists . . . , a Jewish community leader, and a pro-Israeli speaker."

CAMPUS "HATE SPEECH" CODES

This pattern of "hate speech" laws being used to target minority viewpoints also has been evident in the enforcement of campus "hate speech" codes. In 1974, in a move aimed at the National Front, the British National Union of Students (NUS) adopted a resolution that representatives of "openly racist and fascist organizations" were to be prevented from speaking on campuses. The rule had been designed in large part to stem an increase in campus anti-Semitism. Following the UN's cue, however, some British students deemed Zionism a form of racism, and in 1975 they invoked the NUS resolution to disrupt speeches by Israelis, including the Israeli ambassador to Great Britain. The intended target of the NUS resolution, the right-wing National Front, applauded this result. The NUS itself became disenchanted by this and other unintended consequences of its resolution and repealed it in 1977.

The British experience has some parallels under campus "hate speech" codes in the United States. The University of Michigan code was in effect from April 1988 until October 1989, when it was declared unconstitutional in a lawsuit brought by the ACLU. Because of the lawsuit, the university was forced to disclose information about how its code had been enforced, information that otherwise would have been unavailable to the public. Even during the short time that the Michigan code was in effect, there were more than twenty cases of whites charging blacks with racist speech. In only two cases was speech punished on the ground that it was racist, in contrast with being discriminatory on other grounds. And in both such cases, the punished speech was communicated by or on behalf of black students. In one case, a black student was punished for using the term "white trash" in conversation with a white student. The second case arose from a faculty-led small-group discussion at the beginning of a preclinical dentistry course to "identify concerns of students." One student said that he had heard, from his minority roommate, that minority students had a difficult time in the course and were not treated fairly. The faculty member, who was black, complained that the student was accusing her of racism.

Moreover, the only student who was subjected to the burden and stigma of a full-fledged formal disciplinary proceeding under the Michigan rule, as opposed to a more informal resolution process, was an African-American social work graduate student accused of homophobic and sexist expression. The charges stemmed from a research class, in which the student conveyed his belief that homosexuality is a disease and that he intended to develop a counseling plan for changing gay clients to straight, a view that spurred heated debates with his classmates. In seeking clemency for the punishment that was imposed on him after the hearing, the student asserted that the charges were "pretextual" and that he had been singled out because of his race, as well as his political views. He wrote that the complaining students "knew that a black student would have no chance of winning a favorable decision against such charges. These charges will haunt me for the rest of my life. .... [T]hey will be used against me to prevent me from becoming a certified Social Worker."

Indeed, even one of the preeminent proponents of campus rules barring "hate speech," law professor Charles Lawrence, himself recognized the risk that such rules would be invoked disproportionately against African Americans and members of other traditionally oppressed groups. He explicitly charged that other university rules were being used to silence antiracist expression but not racist expression. Accordingly, to avert this predictable problem, Lawrence advocated writing "hate speech" laws in such a way that they would not protect "persons who were vilified on the basis of their membership in dominant majority groups." As the next chapter discusses, this strategy—which also has been endorsed by other prominent proponents of American "hate speech" laws—would cause more problems than it would solve.

CANADA'S TREATMENT OF MISOGYNISTIC PORNOGRAPHY AS A FORM OF "HATE SPEECH"

The predictable problem of officials' enforcing "hate speech" laws to suppress minority views and speakers also resulted from a specific type of "hate speech" law enforced by our Canadian neighbors: a law targeting "pornography," as some feminists label sexual expression that is "degrading" or "dehumanizing" to women. In other words, the anti-pornography law that these feminists championed targets a specific subset of "hate speech": speech that conveys misogynistic views through sexual words and images.

In 1992, some Canadian feminists persuaded the Canadian Supreme Court, in a case called *Butler v. The Queen*, to incorporate this concept into Canada's anti-obscenity law. Anti-censorship feminists had long warned that any such legal concept would predictably be used not to advance women's equality or safety but rather to stifle expression on behalf of disempowered groups, including women and LGBT people. Sadly, those predictions were fulfilled. The subjective concepts at the heart of all "hate speech" laws—in this case, "degrading" and "dehumanizing"—empowered police officers, judges, and other officials to target works that were inconsistent with their own values. Some Canadian law enforcement officials and judges indicated that they considered any depiction of same-sex intimacies to inherently satisfy these criteria.

Accordingly, even the Canadian pro-censorship feminist organization that had championed the *Butler* decision was quickly forced to acknowledge *Butler*'s pernicious effects on equality goals. This organization, the Women's Legal Education and Action Fund (LEAF), joined with anti-censorship feminists in 1993 to issue a joint news release that "condemned the use of the *Butler* decision to justify the discriminatory use of laws to harass and intimidate lesbians and gays." The LEAF signatories further conceded that "[s]ince . . . *Butler* . . . Canada Customs, some police forces . . . and some government funders have exploited obscenity law to harass bookstores, artists, and AIDS organizations, sex trade workers, and safe sex educators."

SOCIAL MEDIA BANS ON "HATE SPEECH"

"I'm not so worried about companies censoring Nazis, but I am worried about the . . . unelected bros of Silicon Valley being the judge and jury. . . . I'm worried that, just like Cloudflare CEO Matthew Prince woke up one morning and decided he'd had enough of the *Daily Stormer*, some other CEO might wake up and do the same for Black Lives Matter or antifa."
—Jillian York, Electronic Frontier Foundation

"Those of us who believe that online intermediaries have an important role to play in creating . . . safe social spaces have to acknowledge . . . that, traditionally, the first voices to be silenced in private or public censorship are . . . dissenting voices from the margins."
—New York Law School professor Ari Waldman, expert on cyberharassment and LGBTQ youth

Research into social media platforms' enforcement of their bans on "hate speech" predictably has found that their inevitably vague standards have been enforced inconsistently. National Public Radio (NPR) conducted one such study in 2016. Focusing on Facebook posts "that could be considered hate speech—specifically, attacks against blacks and against whites in the U.S."—NPR concluded that the standards were unevenly enforced, leading to a high percentage of situations where Facebook reversed the initial decisions in both directions: removing some posts that had not been removed initially and restoring others that had been removed.

Although to date Facebook has not publicly revealed its criteria for determining what constitutes impermissible "hate speech," in 2017 ProPublica obtained "a trove of internal [Facebook] documents," which "sheds light on the algorithms" and "the hundreds of rules, drawing elaborate distinctions," that Facebook's "army of censors" uses "to differentiate between hate speech and legitimate political expression." Not surprisingly, these guidelines require subjective judgments, which in turn lead to the inconsistent enforcement actions that NPR flagged. For example, Facebook defines "hate speech" against "migrants" to include "dehumanizing" generalizations about them but not "degrading" generalizations. According to one Facebook document, migrants may be referred to as "filthy," but not as "filth."

In addition to enforcing "hate speech" definitions unpredictably and inconsistently, social media also have been accused of enforcing such definitions to the detriment of minority speakers and dissenting perspectives. ProPublica's 2017 analysis of Facebook's internal documents noted that "at least in some instances, the company's hate-speech rules tend to favor elites and governments over grassroots activists and racial minorities." ProPublica noted that such favoritism serves Facebook's business interests, since it "relies on national governments not to block its services to their citizens."

In 2017, Facebook enforced its "hate speech" policies to censor self-described "queer rights activists" for using words such as "dyke" and "fag." Boston poet and Black Lives Matter activist Didi Delgado deplored "the increasingly common Facebook censorship of black activists," some of whom use the nickname "Racebook."

Kate Klonick, a Ph.D. candidate at Yale Law School, who has been studying tech companies' enforcement of their restrictions on "hate speech" and other disfavored messages, expressed concern that Facebook is "evolving into a place where celebrities, world leaders and other important people" have "disproportionate . . . power to" persuade Facebook to permit certain material to be posted, even if it violates Facebook's rules.

In 2017, a coalition of seventy-seven organizations and individuals advocating civil rights wrote to Facebook to renew complaints, which at least some of them had been raising with it since 2014, that Facebook was engaging in "consistent and disproportionate censorship of . . . users of color . . . when they call out racism." The coalition accused Facebook of using a "double standard" under which Black Lives Matter, Native American, and other racial justice "activists have been censored for political speech and for posting images critical of government officers—including police officers"—while Facebook "failed to prevent . . . violent threats and harassment by white supremacist hate groups" on its platform.

In response, Facebook acknowledged that "too often we get it wrong" and voiced a commitment to improve its handling of "hate speech," including by improving the software it uses to flag such speech. This response prompted the coalition to renew its complaints, stressing that Facebook had "failed to address the modest solutions to racially biased censorship we presented . . . including . . . a streamlined . . . appeals process, [and] increased transparency."

CURRENT TARGETING OF DISFAVORED VIEWS
IN COMPARABLE DEMOCRACIES

I have cited examples from many countries in which "hate speech" laws have been enforced to stifle political dissent and minority speakers. We would expect these patterns in countries with authoritarian political structures or traditions, but what is especially sobering is the extent to which "hate speech" laws have been used to punish and chill dissident views and marginalized individuals and groups even in mature democracies. In each community officials predictably tend to invoke these laws against whatever views and speakers are unpopular in that community at that time.

In Europe, the ideas that recently have been targeted include some that enjoy substantial popular support but that run counter to the prevailing political orthodoxy. A prime example is speech critiquing immigration from predominantly Muslim countries, specifically focusing on aspects of Islam that are seen as conflicting with secular democratic values, including women's rights. Another frequent recent target of European "hate speech" laws is expression that conveys certain traditional religious views, particularly those that consider homosexuality sinful. Although these views are from the right end of the political spectrum, as journalist Glenn Greenwald stressed in 2017, "hate speech laws are used in virtually every country in which they exist . . . to punish . . . a wide range of views that many on the left believe should be permissible, if not outright accepted."

Now I will describe a few more examples of the many recent situations in which European "hate speech" laws have triggered at least complaints, arrests, and investigations—and in some cases also prosecutions and even convictions—due to speech about public matters. These situations spotlight the dangers these laws pose when they are enforced against public officials and public figures. Such enforcement is especially dangerous in a democracy, for as the European Court of Human Rights observed: "[F]reedom of expression is particularly important for political parties and their . . . members. . . . Accordingly, interferences with the freedom of expression of a politician" are singularly problematic.

France: Bob Dylan Criminally Charged Because of Statement in Magazine Interview

In 2013, musician and poet Bob Dylan, winner of the 2016 Nobel Prize for Literature, was charged with "incitement to racial hatred" when he was in France to receive its most prestigious national prize, the "Légion d'Honneur." This charge, which could result in up to one year of imprisonment, arose from Dylan's brief reference to Croatians in a 2012 *Rolling Stone* magazine interview. The allegedly criminal "hate speech" was at the end of Dylan's answer to the interviewer's question about racial discrimination: "If you got a slave master or Klan in your blood, blacks can sense that. . . . Just like Jews can sense Nazi blood and the Serbs can sense Croatian blood." A judge ultimately dismissed the charges against Dylan, but not because his statement was not criminal; rather, the judge concluded that Dylan had not consented to the statement's publication in France, thus relieving him personally of culpability, but not relieving the publisher. French prosecutors accordingly filed criminal "hate speech" charges against *Rolling Stone.*

Britain: European Parliament Candidate Arrested During Campaign Speech for Quoting Winston Churchill

Paul Weston, chairman of the British political party Liberty GB, was arrested while delivering a campaign speech when he was a candidate in the 2014 European elections. He quoted a passage from Winston Churchill's 1899 book *The River War,* conveying Churchill's negative view of what he called "Mohammedanism"; the critique reflected, in part, Churchill's concern about women's rights. As he wrote in the passage that Weston quoted: "The fact that in Mohammedan law every woman must belong to some man as his absolute property—either as a child, a wife, or a concubine— must delay the final extinction of slavery until the faith of Islam has ceased to be a great power among men."

At least half a dozen police officers (according to some press accounts even more) arrived during the speech to investigate the reported "crime"; they questioned Weston, arrested him, searched him, put him in a police van, and drove him to the local police station, where he was imprisoned in a cell for several hours and then charged with "racially aggravated crime," which carries a potential prison sentence of two years. Approximately two months later, the police told Weston that they had decided not to pursue the charges, but they issued an ominously vague warning that "if further significant evidence becomes available at a later date, the decision may be reconsidered."

A strong denunciation of Weston's arrest came from, of all people, his political opponent in the European Parliament election for which Weston had been campaigning: Daniel Hannan, a journalist and Conservative Party politician. As Hannan wrote:

> [A] candidate was arrested for addressing his potential voters. [P]onder that elemental fact. . . . *[A] candidate was arrested for making a hustings speech* . . . I realize that "political arrest" is a strong phrase, but it's hard to think of any other way to describe a candidate for public office being taken into police custody because of objections to the content of his pitch.

Netherlands: Member of Parliament Convicted Because of Question He Asked at Political Rally

Dutch Member of Parliament Geert Wilders, leader of the far-right Party for Freedom, repeatedly has been prosecuted and tried under Dutch "hate speech" laws, but he was not convicted until December 2016. A lawyer for some of the complainants touted a unique feature of this ruling, which many supporters of liberty and democracy would hardly view as cause for celebration: it was "the first" judicial ruling "in the Netherlands that there are limits to what even a politician can say" in terms of proscribed viewpoints. The conviction arose from a 2014 political rally during which Wilders posed the following question to the crowd: "Do you want more or fewer Moroccans in this city and in the Netherlands?" In response, the crowd chanted, "Fewer, fewer."

Denmark: Member of Parliament and Three Other Public Figures Convicted for Criticizing Aspects of Islam

In four recent cases, Denmark's "hate speech" law was enforced against a public official and three public figures for comments that criticized aspects of Islam. The most recent involved artist Firoozeh Bazrafkan, a Danish citizen who was born in Iran as a Muslim, with relatives who still live in Iran. Citing her direct knowledge of "Islamic regimes," Bazrafkan stated: "Islamic codes give men the rights to do whatever they want to women and children." In 2013, an appellate court, over a dissent, pronounced her guilty and sentenced her to a fine of 5,000 kroner (US $900) or a five-day prison term because she had made "statements in which a group of people are mocked and degraded because of their beliefs." Consider the frightening implications of this reasoning. All beliefs are held by people. Therefore, according to the court's rationale, we should not be permitted to critique any beliefs that are held by "a group of people"—at least when the group is defined by characteristics such as religion, race, and gender, which are protected by "hate speech" laws—because that is tantamount to "mock[ing] and degrad[ing]" the group itself.

In three other recent incidents, Danish public figures were convicted for criticizing aspects of Islam, particularly its treatment of women and children. In 2011, Lars Hedegaard, a historian and journalist, was convicted for such statements made in a private setting. The Danish Supreme Court later overturned his conviction not because he had a right to make the statements, but because he had not intended the statements to be published. Jesper Langballe, a Lutheran pastor and Member of Parliament, was convicted because of statements he made in a newspaper op-ed that defended Hedegaard. Lars Kragh Andersen, a political activist, was convicted for writing an article saying that "Muslim men . . . abuse and kill their daughters."

All of these cases present a troubling pattern of "hate speech" laws being enforced to bar meaningful public discussion about important public policy controversies.

Austria: Citizen's Facebook Post Criticizing Public Official
Is Deemed "Hate Speech" That Facebook Must Delete Worldwide

It is troubling enough that "hate speech" laws suppress statements about public issues by politicians and other public figures, as in the foregoing cases. Worse yet is when public officials are shielded from critical statements about them and their actions by the citizens to whom they are accountable. Yet that is exactly what happened recently in Austria. In 2017, the Austrian Court of Appeal affirmed a lower court ruling that anonymous Facebook posts criticizing Austria's Green Party leader, Eva Glawischnig, constituted illegal "hate speech." The posts called her "miese Volksverräterin" and "korrupte[s] Trampel," which roughly translate as "lousy traitor" and "corrupt bumpkin." Both courts concurred that Facebook had to delete these "hate postings" and all verbatim repostings globally.

Exemplifying the inevitable subjectivity in enforcing "hate speech" laws, the appellate court said that these postings went beyond "political comment" and "legitimate criticism," which would have constituted protected free speech, but instead "were aimed at insulting and vilifying [the Green Party leader] personally," rendering them illegal. Just think about how that "standard" might be applied to statements made by and about politicians in the United States.

CHILLING EFFECT

As if all of the outright suppression under "hate speech" laws were not problematic enough, they also have had the chilling effect that one would expect from such unduly vague, broad laws. University of Virginia political science professor Gerard Alexander observed that in the enforcement of European "hate speech" laws "[t]he most serious chill is not of fringe racists but of mainstream moderates and conservatives." He explained that this chilling impact flows from the devastating, perhaps irreparable, adverse consequences of any "brushes" with these laws: "[A]n increasing number of European intellectuals, politicians, journalists, and even scholars have had uncomfortable and expensive brushes with speech laws. In many cases, their reputation is tarnished; afterward their Wikipedia entry, so to speak, is never complete without mention of the official investigation for bigotry."

Similarly, the dissenting Canadian Supreme Court justices who voted in 1990 to strike down Canada's "hate speech" legislation as violating that country's free speech guarantee warned of its dangerous chilling effect on mainstream discourse. They noted that while the "hate speech" law "may pose little deterrent to a convinced hate-monger who may welcome the publicity it brings; it may, however, deter the ordinary individual." Of course, we can never know how much speech we lose due to self-censorship, but these dissenting justices suggested likely examples that are all too plausible in light of the actual enforcement record of "hate speech" laws in Canada and other democratic countries, as I recount throughout this book:

> Novelists may steer clear of controversial characterizations of ethnic characteristics, such as Shakespeare's portrayal of Shylock in *The Merchant of Venice*. Scientists may well think twice before researching and publishing results of research suggesting difference between ethnic or racial groups. . . . [E]ven political debate on crucial issues such as immigration, educational language rights, foreign ownership and trade may be tempered.

THE SLIPPERY SLOPE

Defenders of the "hate speech" laws in other developed democracies often note that these countries have not slid all the way down the proverbial "slippery slope" into the kinds of censorship that we see in authoritarian regimes. But there has been some substantial slippage, as I have illustrated, and as human rights activists in other democratic countries have complained. I want to make four final points in this chapter about how the scope of "hate speech" laws has been steadily expanded.

First, as we have seen, "hate speech" laws have often been invoked against general statements of opinion about public policy matters. Most prominent proponents of "hate speech" laws in the United States oppose using these laws to punish such statements, maintaining that "hate speech" laws should target only direct personal insults.

Second, the scope of "hate speech" laws has been legislatively expanded in various ways around the world, including by broadening the groups about whom hateful, discriminatory expression is illegal, and by increasing the penalties. The pioneering law review articles that advocated "hate speech" laws in the United States all confined their proposed laws specifically to racist speech, arguing that the legacy of slavery and Jim Crow make it a uniquely toxic form of "hate speech." Can we imagine resisting the powerful arguments, though, that multiple other forms of discrimination have been similarly entrenched and poisonous in their own ways? As the next chapter explains, "hate speech" laws in other countries not only outlaw speech about a broad spectrum of groups and characteristics, ranging (in alphabetical order) from "age" to "social status," but some of them also contain sweeping catch-all provisions outlawing, for instance, "hate speech" against "any other group."

Third, "hate speech" laws have undergone what one Danish critic has called "scope-creep": enforcing officials (mis)interpret such laws to function as blasphemy laws. Some "hate speech" laws explicitly bar speech that targets people because of their religious beliefs. Under "hate speech" laws that shield "religious beliefs," criticism of certain Islamic beliefs has been treated as "hate speech" against Muslims. Many Western democratic countries, as well as human rights organizations, have rejected such provisions because they effectively resurrect the blasphemy laws that have been widely repudiated as violating both freedom of speech and religious liberty. For example, in opposing efforts by the Organization of the Islamic Conference to outlaw "defamation of religion" as an international human rights violation, a coalition of human rights organizations wrote: "[H]uman rights . . . protect individuals from harm, but not beliefs from critical inquiry." For these reasons, it is especially problematic that some enforcing authorities have construed "hate speech" laws that do *not* contain provisions protecting religious beliefs as if they did. Recall, for example, the Danish case I described earlier in this chapter.

Fourth, "hate speech" laws encourage government to enact additional laws, which punish speech that conveys other kinds of "offensive" ideas, beyond hateful, discriminatory ideas. In 2012, British journalist Jerome Taylor wrote, "in recent years we have increasingly begun to criminalise the offensive."

For example, new variations on "hate speech" laws have proliferated in European and other democratic countries: laws criminalizing statements about certain historical events. These began with laws criminalizing Holocaust denial, and they have been succeeded by laws barring certain statements about other genocides and human rights abuses.

In 1993, Princeton professor Bernard Lewis, a noted expert on the Ottoman Empire, was interviewed by France's *Le Monde* newspaper about the mass murder of Armenians in Turkey during World War I. He of course acknowledged that these murders had been committed, but questioned whether they resulted from a predetermined plan to exterminate an ethnic group, which is the legal definition of "genocide." For raising this question, Lewis was subjected to not only a criminal prosecution but also three civil complaints. He was found culpable in one of the civil suits but not in any of the other proceedings.

These legal proceedings against Lewis underscore both of the key problems with all "hate speech" laws that this chapter has discussed: their inevitable overbreadth and vagueness. I assume that even most proponents of such laws would not support their enforcement against the kind of opinion Lewis voiced, reflecting his good-faith scholarly research and judgment. Moreover, the differing rulings in the four cases against him, all arising out of the very same expression, furnish yet another illustration of such laws' unavoidable vagueness, leading to inconsistent and arbitrary enforcement.

In 2004, France enacted the "Lellouche law," which expanded the concept of criminal "hate speech" to include expression aimed at "a person or a group of persons on the basis of . . . affiliation with a . . . nation." The stated aim was to curb rising anti-Semitism and anti-Arab xenophobia. Nevertheless, it has been invoked repeatedly to punish speech that criticizes certain Israeli government policies, including advocacy of boycotting Israeli products. The law's critics have noted that if it had been in effect at the time, it would have outlawed advocacy of boycotting South Africa's former apartheid regime. The same law has been proposed in other countries as well, including Belgium and Canada.

* * *

In this chapter I have illustrated the intractable problems of vagueness and overbreadth that plague "hate speech" laws, underscoring why the Supreme Court has insisted that any law regulating speech about public issues must be written narrowly and precisely. Despite their wide variations in language and scope, "hate speech" laws uniformly vest enforcing officials with enormous discretionary power, and consistently have been enforced to suppress unpopular views and speakers, including political dissent and minority speakers. Moreover, such laws have chilled even more expression, including mainstream political views. These problems beset the enforcement of "hate speech" laws even in democratic nations. Finally, even if a "hate speech" law were written relatively narrowly, it would be "the worst of both worlds"; it still would repose great discretionary power in enforcing officials due to its inherent vagueness, while not meaningfully reducing the harms that constitutionally protected "hate speech" is feared to cause.

In the next chapter, I explore the multiple challenges that the drafters of any "hate speech" law must address, by drawing upon the language that is contained in many such laws from many countries. My goal is to demonstrate concretely the intrinsic problems of vagueness and overbreadth that singularly characterize "hate speech" laws.

CHAPTER FIVE

Is It Possible to Draft a "Hate Speech" Law That Is Not Unduly Vague or Overbroad?

"It is technically impossible to write an anti-speech code that cannot be twisted against speech nobody means to bar. It has been tried and tried and tried."

—Congresswoman Eleanor Holmes Norton

IN PRIOR CHAPTERS, I have explained why "hate speech" laws are plagued by vagueness and overbreadth, and why those problems pose virtually insurmountable challenges. But is it possible to write a "hate speech" law that is *not* unduly vague and overbroad? It is one thing to advocate for such a law in the abstract, but something else entirely to draft a "hate speech" law that contains acceptably clear, sensible, and narrow criteria. Drawing upon the myriad "hate speech" laws that have been enacted or proposed, this chapter lays out the various elements that such laws include and examines the questions they raise and the problems they pose. This analysis illuminates the impossibility of drafting a "hate speech" law, extending government's regulatory power beyond the emergency test, in a way that coherently defines and constrains such power.

WHAT CONSTITUTIONALLY PROTECTED "HATE SPEECH" SHOULD A "HATE SPEECH" LAW FORBID?

Existing "hate speech" laws differ widely in terms of the personal characteristics they protect. The European Union's definition of illegal "hate speech" contains a typical listing: "race, colour, religion, descent or national or ethnic origin." Other laws delineate many additional characteristics, including (in alphabetical order) age, class, family origin, family situation, financial status, gender, gender identity, handicap, ideology, illness, intellectual disability, lack of religious belief, language, mental disability, nationality, occupation, pregnancy, property status, sexual orientation, and social status. Some "hate speech" laws are essentially all-encompassing, containing such catch-all provisions as "any distinguishing characteristic" or "any personal circumstances" of individuals. A New Jersey court recently enforced a state law including such open-ended language to punish expression criticizing an individual for being a vegetarian and for lacking athletic ability. What is the "correct" list of such characteristics?

Beyond the question of which of these various characteristics should and should not be included in a "hate speech" law, there is a more fundamental underlying question, which I addressed in Chapter 4: How can an enumeration of protected personal characteristics successfully steer between these two problematic alternatives: being unconstitutionally underinclusive, thus impermissibly punishing speech about some groups but not others; and being unconstitutionally overinclusive, thus unjustifiably prohibiting speech that is valuable or at least poses no realistic danger of contributing to serious harm?

Another complication arises from the question whether "hate speech" laws should punish speech that criticizes beliefs as well as characteristics. Some "hate speech" laws expressly treat speech that disparages certain beliefs as equivalent to speech that disparages individuals who hold those beliefs. Some such laws, for example, extend to speech that disparages "religious beliefs," "political beliefs," and even "opinions" more generally. A special problem that arises from these laws is that they could be understood to bar criticism even of the very beliefs that "hate speech" laws seek to suppress: hateful, discriminatory beliefs. Recall one example that Chapter 1 noted: France imposed a substantial fine on an LGBT rights activist under a "hate speech" law for labeling the leader of a group opposing same-sex marriage as a "homophobe."

Still another complex consideration is whether "hate speech laws" should punish statements about certain historical events. For example, many countries have outlawed Holocaust denial and other statements about the Holocaust, essentially on the rationale that such speech is tantamount to anti-Semitic "hate speech." As Noam Chomsky commented, though: "It is a poor service to the memory of the victims of the Holocaust to adopt a central doctrine of their murderers." Some countries also have outlawed speech about other historical war crimes and human rights violations. For example, Spain punishes with imprisonment of up to four years "[p]ublicly denying, trivializing or exalting . . . genocide, crimes against humanity or [crimes] against persons and property protected in . . . armed conflict." In the United States, by analogy, we could reasonably anticipate political pressures to extend "hate speech" laws to speech that conveys controversial views about genocide and other gross human rights abuses that mar our history, including against Native Americans and enslaved Africans and their descendants.

WHAT SHOWING OF HARM SHOULD SUCH A LAW REQUIRE?

"Hate speech" laws differ in the types of harm they seek to prevent. Some expand on the tort law concepts of individual and group defamation by punishing speech that "insults" individuals or groups, thus harming their dignity and reputation. Others expand on the tort law concept of intentionally inflicting emotional distress by outlawing speech that distresses people it disparages. Still others expand on the concept of incitement (though without complying with the emergency principle), by proscribing speech that might promote hatred, hostility, or discrimination, or contribute to possible violent or other illegal conduct.

Some "hate speech" laws don't require any evidence that the proscribed speech actually contributes to any harm, or is likely to do so. They impose categorical bans on speech conveying the forbidden messages without requiring *any* showing of actual, likely, or even possible harm. Article 4 of the U.N. Convention on the Elimination of All Forms of Racial Discrimination (CERD), for example, requires signatories to adopt this sweeping type of "hate speech" law, absolutely outlawing "all dissemination of ideas based on racial superiority or hatred" without requiring any showing that the speech at issue in any particular situation will have a negative effect. (Many nations that ratified CERD did so with reservations to this provision, citing countervailing free speech concerns.)

Existing "hate speech" laws are all over the lot on this question, punishing expression that is deemed to satisfy the following criteria, among many others: "[constitutes] any call for . . . hatred, or any form of intolerance"; "assaults the human dignity of others by insulting, maliciously maligning, or defaming"; "creates a climate of hate or prejudice, which may, in turn, foster the commission of hate crimes"; "degrades"; "demeans"; "[constitutes] disrespectful public discourse"; "encourage[s], promote[s], or incite[s] hatred, . . . hostility, discrimination or violence"; "expose[s] to hatred, persecution or contempt"; "has potential to stir hatred"; "has the effect of violating someone's dignity"; "imputes to another person [or] a group of persons . . . such conduct, or characteristics that may discredit them in the face of public opinion"; "[is] inflaming of hatred and intolerance"; "infringe[s] . . . dignity . . . through humiliation, contempt or discredit"; "injur[es]"; "insults [or] mocks"; "mocks or scorns"; "[constitutes] offensive expression, [a] contemptuous term or invective not based on fact"; "preaches . . . hostility . . . or discrimination"; "promotes feelings of ill will and enmity"; "provokes a feeling of hostility or rejection"; "ridicules or despises"; "stigmatizes"; "vilifies or mocks"; or "wound[s] . . . religious or racial feelings."

Given that "hate speech" laws by definition don't require harm that complies with the emergency test, what less demanding standard would be appropriate? Are some of the posited harms too difficult to demonstrate with objective evidence? Are some tantamount to mere disapproval of the message's idea?

In the Skokie case, the lower federal court suggested that two asserted harms that the government feared would flow from the neo-Nazis' expression could not constitute permissible justifications for restricting the proposed demonstration. First, the court reasoned that the asserted harm of group libel—speech that damages the reputation of a group—was analogous to the now-repudiated concept of "seditious libel," which prohibited speech that might generate "disrespect for and hatred towards the government and public officials." Although there is a special democratic danger in suppressing speech that criticizes officials, it is similarly problematic to suppress speech because it criticizes groups of individuals, for such speech can also have significant public policy implications.

Second, the court noted the problems that would arise if it permitted suppression of the neo-Nazis' speech due to the asserted "psychological trauma" that their speech might cause to potential observers. It explained that determining "the psychological trauma which [racial slurs] may cause" is highly speculative, since it is "difficult to distinguish a person who suffers actual psychological trauma from one who is only highly offended, and . . . speech may not be punished merely because it offends."

In the same vein, Northwestern University Communication Studies professor Franklyn Haiman pointed out that "[i]n a suit for emotional distress arising out of the Skokie incident, a Holocaust survivor, . . . who testified that the sight of marching Nazis would evoke intolerably painful memories of the execution of his parents, was found to have gone willingly to monitor other demonstrations by the neo-Nazis in the Chicago area." Haiman concluded that this survivor's opposition to the Skokie march was "apparently motivated more by anger than by pain." While Haiman did "not denigrate the anger," he stressed that it is a distinct psychological state. And, I might add, it is a psychological state that the Supreme Court has expressly held can never justify suppressing speech. To the contrary, the Court famously declared that "free speech . . . may indeed best serve its high purpose when it . . . stirs people to anger." This is so because "a function of free speech under our system of government is to invite dispute" about public issues and "[s]peech . . . may . . . have profound unsettling effects as it presses for acceptance of an idea."

Additional questions about drafting the harm element in a "hate speech" law concern how likely the harm must be to materialize and how direct and imminent the connection must be between the speech and the harm. Under the emergency principle, speech may be punished only if it directly causes imminent serious harm. Under "hate speech" laws, though, speech is punished merely for its harmful tendency. Is there any persuasive justification for reinstating the long-discredited bad tendency test in the realm of "hate speech"?

Another critical question is what mental state should be required to punish a speaker. Many "hate speech" laws require no specific mental state. Some do specify such an element, but they range across the spectrum: from a strict liability standard, to a negligence standard, to a recklessness standard, to a knowledge standard, to a specific intent standard. What is the "proper" standard?

The strict liability approach is too often enforced or advocated on college campuses, considering only the complainant's perception of the challenged speech without regard to the speaker's mental state. For example, faculty members have been punished, and even fired, merely for uttering racially or ethnically derogatory terms during class discussions, even though they did so to make pedagogically pertinent points, rather than to convey individually targeted insults, and even when they did so specifically in the context of condemning discrimination against the disparaged people.

One prominent example is Brandeis University professor Donald Hindley, who was found guilty of racial harassment and had a monitor placed in his classes because he explained what the term "wetbacks" connotes, and why it is offensive, in his Latin American Politics course. Another example is Kenneth Hardy, who lost his position as an adjunct instructor at Jefferson Community College because of a student complaint that the N-word and the word "bitch" had been used in his "Introduction to Interpersonal Communication" course in a class concerning "language and social constructivism, where the students examined how language is used to marginalize minorities and other oppressed groups in society." As a class exercise, Hardy solicited from students examples of "words that have historically served the interests of the dominant culture," which generated multiple suggestions by students, including the two terms at issue. It is not clear whether

Hardy himself even uttered those terms. When Hardy brought a lawsuit against the college for wrongful discharge, the federal appellate court held that the college had violated his First Amendment rights.

What should the government have to show about the potential connection between the speech and the feared harm, and about the speaker's mental state, that would warrant punishing the speaker and suppressing the speech even though it does not meet the emergency standard? What requirements would suffice to ensure that the government isn't punishing speech simply because it opposes the ideas themselves?

SHOULD THE SIZE AND NATURE OF THE AUDIENCE MATTER?

Should a "hate speech" law require that the forbidden speech specifically target a single individual or a small group of individuals, or should it also punish generalized expressions of ideas, including in a lecture, media interview, website, or publication? Some "hate speech" laws specify that to be punishable the speech must be communicated in a public setting, but others apply even to speech in a private setting. For example, Austria's "hate speech" legislation extends to speech that is uttered "in front of several people," which could occur in someone's home, even among family members. Cyprus's "hate speech" law extends to expression in a "private place" if it "may be heard by any person in a public place." Ireland's law expressly encompasses speech that occurs even "inside a private residence" if it "can be heard or seen by persons outside the residence." Most sweepingly, France's "hate speech" laws expressly extend to "non-public" communications. German courts have gone so far as to uphold a three-month prison sentence that was imposed on a historian for statements he made about Nazi history in a private letter addressed and sent to another historian.

In the United States and elsewhere, judges recognize that communications privacy is a prerequisite for freedom of speech. As George Orwell's classic dystopian novel *1984* so vividly demonstrated, if we fear that "Big Brother is Watching" our conversations, that will prompt self-censorship. Former Supreme Court Justice Thurgood Marshall memorably captured this concern when he declared, on behalf of a unanimous Court: "If the First Amendment means anything, it means that a state has no business telling a man, sitting alone in his own house, what books he may read or what films he may watch." Surely it also means that a state has no business telling a person, sitting with someone in her/his own house, what s/he may or may not say—except in the limited situations when such expression satisfies the emergency test, for example by conveying a punishable threat. But "hate speech" laws by definition are not so limited.

SHOULD THE IDENTITIES OF THE SPEAKER OR THE TARGETS OF THE SPEECH MATTER?

Some prominent proponents of "hate speech" laws maintain that they should not apply neutrally to all targets of the speech. To the contrary, these advocates maintain that such laws should protect only relatively disempowered individuals or groups, but not others. For example, law professor Charles Lawrence's influential article advocating campus "hate speech" codes maintained that such codes should not protect "persons who were vilified on the basis of their membership in dominant majority groups." If we consider the United States as a whole, presumably this would mean that "hate speech" could permissibly target straight people but not LGBT people, and Christians but not Muslims or Jews. As for gender, women constitute the majority of the U.S. population, and also of the student body population on many campuses, but men are nonetheless fairly regarded as "dominant" in many important spheres in our society. Therefore, I assume—but am not sure—that Lawrence and other proponents of more selective "hate speech" laws would contend that "hate speech" could permissibly target men, but not women.

The proponents of such selective "hate speech" laws understandably seek remedies for people who are the most frequent targets of "hate speech" and the most vulnerable to its possible harms. Moreover, these selective laws can reduce the enforcement problem I have discussed concerning "hate speech" laws that are more general in scope: that they are too often disproportionately enforced against members of the very minority groups they were designed to protect.

Despite these rationales for selectively defining those who can invoke "hate speech" laws, this approach poses serious difficulties. Most fundamentally, by favoring some speakers and messages over others, such laws violate both free speech and equality concerns. As the Supreme Court noted in striking down a city law that selectively barred "hate speech" only against some groups and not others: "[The government] has no . . . authority to license one side of a debate to fight freestyle, while requiring the other to follow Marquis [sic] of Queensberry rules."

This selective approach is also highly problematic in practice. Consider the following complexities: Since all of us have multiple personal characteristics, how do we account for such "intersectionality"? What if a black male disparages a white female? What if the speaker was relatively vulnerable due to other personal characteristics, such as gender identity or disability? And aside from personal characteristics, should we ignore other factors that might be relevant in assessing the pertinent power hierarchy, such as occupation or education? Suppose a white man who never made it to college disparages a black man with a Ph.D.?

And in assessing which individuals or groups are relatively powerful or marginalized, what is the pertinent community? Do we consider the United States as a whole or the local community? After all, the identity of "dominant majority groups" often varies from one community to another. How should such a law apply to communities that predominantly consist of groups that are minorities in the United States as a whole? When the neo-Nazis sought to march in Skokie, Illinois, that community was predominantly Jewish, and as the facts of the case indicated, the Jewish residents wielded considerable political influence. Should they therefore be regarded as a "dominant majority group" that would be disqualified from protection under proposed selective "hate speech" laws when enforced in Skokie? And what if an African-American student at a historically black college disparages a white student on campus? Depending on how such questions are answered, we would have radically different conclusions about who actually wields power, and who is actually vulnerable, in any particular scenario.

In sum, selective "hate speech" laws magnify problems that are inherent in all "hate speech" laws; by explicitly authorizing enforcement that is unabashedly discriminatory based on both viewpoint and identity, they squarely conflict with core notions of both liberty and equality. Likewise, these selective laws pose heightened vagueness problems, compounding the resulting arbitrary enforcement problems.

SHOULD OTHER CONTEXTUAL FACTORS BE TAKEN INTO ACCOUNT?

Another complicated question is whether and, if so, how various contextual factors should be taken into account. Potentially relevant contextual factors include, for example, academic settings, media reports, and commentary about "hate speech."

In the academic setting, for example, should "hate speech" rules apply more or less forcefully in classrooms than in other places? Various "hate speech" codes at colleges and universities take diametrically opposing positions on this question, some placing especially severe restrictions on "hate speech" in classrooms and others exempting classrooms from such restrictions. How should academic freedom concerns affect this issue?

As for media reports, in a case under Sweden's "hate speech" legislation, the Swedish courts held a TV station culpable for a program in which white nationalists were interviewed and voiced their racist views. Even though the interviewer did not endorse those views, the Swedish courts held that the station had violated the law because it disseminated the discriminatory message. Ultimately, the European Court of Human Rights overturned that ruling, concluding that when media serve as conduits for other people's views, media should be immune from liability. This Swedish case illustrates that a legal regime could opt for either approach: either incentivizing media to exclude "hate speech" by holding them culpable for any such expression that they transmit; or else incentivizing media to serve, in effect, as "common carriers," permitting all expression to be aired, even if it constitutes otherwise prohibited "hate speech." As we saw in Chapter 1, similar issues arise in the context of social media and other online intermediaries. Which approach is preferable?

Similar problems arise in the context of commentary about "hate speech." What if the hateful message is conveyed for purposes not of propagating its message but, to the contrary, undermining that message? Examples would include quoting the "hate speech" in order to criticize it, or to seek support for those whom it disparaged, or to mock it through humor or satire. As I discuss in Chapter 7, social media have enforced their "hate speech" bans to bar people who have been disparaged by "hate speech" from sharing the hateful messages even for such constructive purposes.

ADDITIONAL COMPLICATIONS

Some "hate speech" laws expressly articulate affirmative defenses, while others expressly exclude certain affirmative defenses. Ireland, for example, protects otherwise punishable "hate speech" if it has "serious literary, artistic, political, or scientific value," whereas Germany's legislation specifies that "proof of truth . . . shall not exclude punishment." When a statute doesn't explicitly either authorize or preclude a particular affirmative defense, it is up to enforcing authorities, including courts, to decide whether or not to recognize any. Many courts have rejected a range of proffered affirmative defenses. As we saw in Chapters 1 and 4, for example, there have been many cases in which Christian and Muslim religious leaders have been prosecuted and convicted under "hate speech" laws for conveying their religious beliefs, including by quoting from their religion's sacred texts. In these cases, the enforcing authorities rejected affirmative defenses based on sincerely held religious beliefs.

Yet another complication concerns speech by public officials and political candidates. Should they be exempt from "hate speech" laws because of the importance of hearing their views? As illustrated by instances discussed in the previous chapters, "hate speech" laws regularly have targeted speech by public officials and candidates in many democratic countries. To deter them from conveying their views deprives voters of important information about their opinions and character. On the other hand, if officials and candidates are exempted from a "hate speech" law that applies to their constituents, that creates a power imbalance, which is at odds with popular sovereignty. The European Court of Human Rights has taken inconsistent positions on this issue. In some cases, it has held that politicians' speech should be especially protected, given its unique importance for democracy, whereas in others it has held that politicians' speech should be especially restricted, on the ground that it has enhanced capacity to cause potential harm.

And then there is the issue of penalties and remedies. Should the law impose punitive sanctions, such as monetary fines or imprisonment, or should it instead take a nonpunitive, educational approach? A number of European countries impose substantial prison terms for "hate speech." For example, French and German "hate speech" laws impose prison terms of up to five years for a first offense. Alternative remedies could include conciliatory steps by the speaker, consistent with the "restorative justice" model. Some judges have devised remedies that aren't spelled out in the statutes, such as requiring the speaker to make financial contributions to organizations that defend the rights of disparaged people. As I discuss in Chapter 8, people who have been disparaged by "hate speech" often prefer to receive a prompt, personalized remedy—including a sincere apology—rather than undergoing the protracted proceedings that are a prerequisite for criminal punishment and also often for civil sanctions.

WHERE DOES THIS LEAVE US?

Taking into account the factors that I have discussed in this chapter, can we identify and describe some hateful, discriminatory speech that is now constitutionally protected, because it does not directly cause specific serious imminent harm, yet nonetheless warrants restriction? And can we do so with sufficient clarity and precision to satisfactorily constrain official discretion and avoid excessive self-censorship? Would any of us be willing to subject our own speech to such a law, as it might be administered by politicians, police, prosecutors, educators, judges, and jurors?

The analysis shows that the very concept of "hate speech" is irreducibly riddled with ambiguity, conflicts, and confusion. Therefore, even if we were willing to depart from the fundamental viewpoint neutrality and emergency principles, any "hate speech" law would still run afoul of fundamental free speech principles because it would be unacceptably vague or overbroad.

I have done my best to track down and read every "hate speech" law that has been enacted or proposed, and have yet to encounter one that avoids the serious flaws that I have identified. For anyone who aspires to draft or discover a "hate speech" law that does so, I am put in mind of Samuel Johnson's famous quip about someone who gets remarried after an unhappy marriage; it reflects the triumph of hope over experience.

Succeeding chapters discuss additional shortcomings that all extant "hate speech" laws share, despite their many variations. As I shall show, they have been ineffective, and perhaps even counterproductive, in reducing the potential harms that are feared to flow from constitutionally protected "hate speech."

CHAPTER SIX

Does Constitutionally Protected "Hate Speech" Actually Cause the Feared Harms?

"[To justify a speech regulation,] the Government [must] demonstrate that the recited harms [of the speech] are real, not merely conjectural, and that the regulation will in fact alleviate these harms in a direct and material way."

—Supreme Court, *U.S. v. National Treasury Employees Union* (1995)

IN PREVIOUS CHAPTERS I explained that "hate speech" laws violate the essential viewpoint neutrality and emergency principles, and also pose special risks of vagueness and overbreadth. For these reasons, such laws endanger freedom of speech (especially for minority perspectives and speakers) and undermine democratic legitimacy. These are compelling reasons to reject "hate speech" laws. But even if such laws didn't pose these problems, we would still have to question whether they actually have the positive effects that their proponents claim. Do "hate speech" laws in fact reduce discrimination, violence, and psychic injuries?

This largely unexamined claim rests on two assumptions: first, that constitutionally protected "hate speech" materially contributes to the feared harms; and second, that "hate speech" laws effectively reduce both the problematic speech and the feared harms. In this chapter and the next I present information that calls each assumption, in turn, into serious question.

The assumption that constitutionally protected "hate speech" significantly contributes to the feared harms is flawed for two reasons. First, there is insufficient evidence that "hate speech" in general plays such a role. Second, there is even less evidence that *constitutionally protected* "hate speech" in particular has such an effect. When proponents of "hate speech" laws cite instances of "hate speech" that, they maintain, are sufficiently harmful to warrant censorship, the examples they offer often satisfy the emergency test and hence are already punishable. Because constitutionally protected "hate speech" by definition does not directly cause specific imminent serious harm, any potential harm it might cause is necessarily more speculative and unpredictable.

TO WHAT EXTENT DOES CONSTITUTIONALLY PROTECTED "HATE SPEECH" CAUSE HARM?

"Many today in the communication-science tradition reject the magic bullet theory of direct, powerful, and uniform changes in attitudes and behaviors caused by messages. Instead, communication is viewed as a complex process . . . , with contingent conditions and mediating variables influencing the chain of causation."
—Communications professor Clay Calvert,
University of Florida

"[I]t is virtually impossible to isolate the effects of the media in the context of other influences, including individuals' demographic

backgrounds and personality characteristics, socialization by family and peer groups, [and] wider cultural influences."
—Sociology professor Ronald Weitzer,
George Washington University

There seems to be a natural tendency to blame expression for antisocial attitudes and conduct. After all, words and images can help to shape ideas and behavior. That is precisely why speech is important. Indeed, having dedicated my life to teaching, speaking, writing, and advocating, I certainly hope and believe that expression can have an impact. But that doesn't mean that we should outlaw speech merely because it *might* have bad effects. As we learned from the rampant censorship of government critics and social justice crusaders under the since-repudiated bad tendency test, such an approach inevitably permits the government to punish speech solely because it disfavors the message or the speaker (even when it doesn't acknowledge this motive).

Psychic or Emotional Harm?

Given that all communications have at least some potential impact on us, it is not surprising that "hate speech" sometimes contributes to psychic, emotional harms to some people whom it disparages. Whether this occurs in any particular situation, however, depends on all the facts and circumstances, including the individual characteristics and circumstances of both the speaker and the disparaged individual. This point was acknowledged even by law professor Richard Delgado, in his important 1982 article advocating a new tort action for "racial insults" because such speech could cause emotional distress. Delgado conceded that "the emotional damage caused" by such insults "is variable and depends on many factors, only one of which is the outrageousness of the insult." Therefore, even such a loathsome epithet as "You damn [N-word]," Delgado acknowledged, should not always be actionable.

Social scientists who specialize in communications have noted that the potential of "hate speech" to contribute to psychic or emotional harms has "not received much empirical investigation," and that "there is little good research evidence of [such] harm." These experts recognize that "there are wide individual differences regarding what constitutes a hurtful message," and that "what speech is considered harmful depends critically on situational variables," including bystanders' reactions, the message's perceived intent, the relationship between the speaker and listener, the topic of discussion, the location of the conversation, the language used, the speaker's and the listener's body language, and tone of voice. In addition, "a great deal of research suggests that social support and certain personality characteristics moderate the effects of stress" that could potentially result from being the target of "hate speech." Reactions of disparaged individuals "are mediated by past experiences, psychological and physical strength, status, needs, [and] goals," among other factors.

A study that started to fill the gap in empirical research on this topic was conducted by Laura Leets of the Stanford University Communication Department. She recruited Jewish and LGBT college students to read several anti-Semitic and homophobic slurs, respectively, and to answer questions about how they would have responded if they had been the targets of these hateful messages. All of the expressions were drawn from actual situations. Strikingly, "a common response" by the student participants was that the "hate speech" would have had "no effect" upon them in either the short run or the long run. Many of the participants in the study expressed the belief that the speaker was motivated by ignorance or insecurity, and therefore should be the object of pity, not anger. Some participants said they would have reacted by calmly responding to the speaker; some said they would have ignored the speaker; and others indicated they would have reacted angrily. While some participants said they would have had negative reactions, hampering their self-esteem at least immediately after the "hate speech," these participants represented only a minority of the group. An especially intriguing aspect of the Leets study was that 83% of the participants viewed silence in response to "hate speech" as an empowered and empowering response, not a weak or passive one. They considered a silent response, including walking away from the disparaging speaker, as taking the higher moral ground.

Key findings of the Leets study have been corroborated by more recent, more extensive data. Especially noteworthy is a recently published annual national survey of incoming first-year college students, which the UCLA Higher Education Research Institute has conducted since 1967. The survey of students entering college in 2015 documented an all-time high among African-American and other minority students in terms of their planned speaking-out and activism against discrimination, both on campus and in the larger community and the political system generally. These responses indicate that the students' overriding reaction to the widely reported recent incidents of "hate speech" and bias crimes has not been depression and withdrawal, but active engagement. As the study's authors concluded: "Recent developments may have signaled to students that a collective sense of belonging and working together to raise important issues on campus and in their communities can lead to change."

I recognize that some of the preceding information focuses on college students, and that hateful speech could have different psychic impacts on others, including those who are less educationally advantaged. As Chapter 8 discusses, there are educational tools for developing everyone's ability to resist the potentially negative effects of hateful speech, and these resources should be widely accessible.

In assessing the psychic and other harm that could potentially result from "hate speech," Northeastern University psychology professor Lisa Feldman Barrett has distinguished "long stretches of simmering stress" from "periodic bouts of stress." As examples of "hate speech" that contributes to the "chronic" or "prolonged" stress that can cause physical as well as psychological harm, she cites "rampant bullying in school or on social media." In contrast, as an example of "hate speech" that "is not bad for your body and brain," and in fact can "be educational," she cites "temporary" exposure to an "odious idea": "There is a difference between . . . a culture of casual brutality and . . . an opinion you strongly oppose." As I explained in Chapter 3, expression that fairly can be characterized as "rampant bullying" would likely constitute targeted harassment, which may be punished consistent with the emergency test.

As Chapter 7 discusses in more detail, research studies have shown that how we perceive or interpret stressful situations, including hearing hateful speech, can substantially alter our psychological and physiological reactions. Therefore, some psychologists argue that the best strategy for both mental and physical health is education about the fact that such speech is not necessarily harmful, and about how to perceive such stressful situations as opportunities for positive personal development. As psychologist Pamela Paresky has observed: "Students who believe that hearing certain words or listening to certain speakers can harm them may . . . succumb to a self-fulfilling prophecy. . . . But it is the belief that words can do harm that causes the harm, not the words themselves." A *New York Times* article summarized the pertinent research as follows: "You can view stress as something that is wreaking havoc on your body . . . or as something that is giving you the strength and energy to overcome adversity. . . . *In a tough situation, stress can make you stronger.*"

Even if constitutionally protected "hate speech" does directly cause psychic or emotional harm in some cases, that still would not warrant censoring it. As noted in prior chapters, the core viewpoint neutrality principle means that government may not punish speech about public issues, including "hate speech," solely because it might have some negative psychic or emotional impact on some people. Given the endless array of speech about public concerns that could have such an impact, any other rule would largely muzzle democratic discourse.

Generating Hateful Attitudes and Actions?

Does "hate speech" foster hateful and discriminatory attitudes and actions among those who hear it? A comprehensive review of social science research about potential links between media messages and audience behavior concluded that the effects on audience behavior are "weak and affect only a small percentage of" audience members. The conclusion that expression has only a limited, virtually unascertainable impact on any audience member's later actions has been confirmed by social science research on the impact of two controversial types of expression: depictions of violence and "pornography."

The Supreme Court recently had occasion to review one aspect of the social science literature on the effects—or, actually, noneffects—of violent speech. In a 2011 decision, the Court struck down a California law restricting the sale of violent videogames to children, which was based on fears that children who viewed such videos would be influenced to act violently. However, not a single study showed that exposure to violent videogames caused minors to act aggressively.

Recognizing the attenuated and unpredictable effect of expression on subsequent conduct, courts have consistently held that, except in the rare situation in which the emergency principle is satisfied, antisocial acts, including violence, cannot be attributed to the actor's exposure to certain expression. Courts have rejected such claims concerning many mass media productions, including television, films, music, websites, and videogames. In 2002, for example, a federal appellate court upheld the lower court's dismissal of a claim that the producers of certain violent media works could be deemed even partially responsible for school shootings committed by a teenager who had watched them.

If creators and distributors of expressive material were held liable for antisocial acts that some individuals committed after viewing the material, then no work would be safe—certainly neither the Bible nor the Qu'ran, which both have been accused of instigating countless individual and mass crimes. Stressing the necessarily varied reactions that individual audience members have to different messages, the court in the school shootings case explained:

> [I]deas ... which may drive some people to violence or ruin, may inspire others to feats of excellence or greatness. . . . Atrocities have been committed in the name of many of civilization's great religions, intellectuals, and artists, yet [we do] not hold those whose ideas inspired the crimes to answer for such acts. To do so would be to allow the . . . misfits . . . to declare what the rest of the country can and cannot read, watch and hear.

As the British writer Kenan Malik has noted, in explaining his opposition to "hate speech" laws: "Racists are, of course, influenced by racist talk. It is they, however, who bear responsibility for translating racist talk into racist action. Ironically, for all the talk of using free speech responsibly, the real consequence of the demand for censorship is to moderate the responsibility of individuals for their actions."

THE IMPORTANCE OF COUNTERSPEECH

The influential early articles that advocated the enactment of "hate speech" laws in the United States, by law professors Richard

Delgado, Mari Matsuda, and Charles Lawrence, were published several decades ago. Although these articles stressed the psychic and emotional harms resulting from racist speech, they attributed such harms in substantial part to the media's and the public's response—or, more accurately, lack of response—to such speech. They charged that racist speech received scant public or media attention, and failed to spur sufficient counterspeech by government or campus officials, or by other community members. They suggested that people disparaged by racist speech suffered at least as much from this lack of attention and support from others as from the racist speech itself, and accordingly they endorsed counterspeech as an essential remedy.

For example, in his 1982 article, Delgado wrote that people disparaged by racist speech experienced "the sense of helplessness that leads to psychological harm"; to counter these negative effects, he advocated "communicating to the perpetrator and to society that [racial insults] will not be tolerated." Although he also advocated a new "hate speech" tort for racial insults, he acknowledged that if there was significant "social pressure" against hateful expression, "prejudiced persons may even refrain from discriminatory behavior to escape social disapproval."

Similarly, Matsuda's 1989 article stressed the harm caused by "state silence" in response to hateful speech, which "offer[s] legitimation" for it. She noted that such "[o]fficial tolerance of racist speech" is especially harmful in the university setting, because the "targets . . . perceive the university as taking sides through inaction." Matsuda also commended counterspeech as an effective response to hateful speech. Charles Lawrence's 1990 article advocating campus "hate speech" codes likewise stressed that society had not sufficiently listened to people disparaged by hateful speech, making them feel that "we have abandoned them," therefore increasing the suffering they experience. Lawrence emphasized the positive impact that counterspeech could have, while charging us all to "ask ourselves whether . . . we have been forceful enough in our personal condemnation of ideas we abhor."

While our society still faces serious challenges in remedying hatefulness and discrimination, the specific problems that were so salient for these influential "hate speech" law advocates—the dearth of attention to and support for targets of "hate speech"—are now no longer operative. Although social media have been flooded with various forms of "hate speech," both social media themselves and mainstream media are also awash in counterspeech; they widely report incidents of "hate speech," presenting them as serious social problems, and condemning them as "un-American." To cite just two of many possible examples, the *New York Times* carries a regular feature entitled "This Week in Hate," and ProPublica and other media outlets have pooled their resources to create a "Documenting Hate" project.

In what it called "the first comprehensive review of hate speech at higher education institutions since the 2016 election," a September 2017 *BuzzFeed News* article reported the proverbial good news/bad news scenario. The bad news was that it "confirmed 154 total ["hate speech"] incidents at more than 120 campuses across the country," but the good news was that "[c]olleges typically responded to bias incidents quickly and to the satisfaction of their students. . . . In nearly every case, university presidents sent off mass emails condemning the hate speech."

Hateful, discriminatory expression and actions now are swiftly and strongly condemned by government officials, community leaders, social media campaigns, and members of the disparaged groups and organizations that champion their rights. Such condemnation is leveled not only against intentional, explicitly hateful expression, but also against unwittingly insensitive expression. As one commentator has observed: "For a politician or a journalist . . . to be labeled racist is usually equivalent to the end of their public career." Indeed, in 2017, a (white) Florida state senator was forced to resign after he used a racist slur in a private conversation with several other state legislators, for which he abjectly apologized. In another recent example, after HBO host Bill Maher's use of the N-word for attempted comic purposes, for which he also promptly apologized, HBO was pressured to fire him.

Two British scholars, Dennis J. Baker and Lucy Zhao, have observed that if anyone is marginalized by hateful, discriminatory speech these days it is those who express hateful opinions. They conclude that "the message that we are all equal . . . is very visible in Western democracies [and] . . . is backed up with a mass of . . . laws." As a consequence, "media scrutiny, public shaming, and strong majority attitudes" should "prevent denigrating expression from making those denigrated feel as less than full members of society." Communications scholar Cherian George, whose 2016 book analyzed "hate speech" laws in multiple countries, concurs with Baker and Zhao, concluding that "in a society with strong anti-discrimination laws, hate speech may not be able to inflict much harm." He even postulated that the violent demonstrations that took place in many European countries, protesting cartoons depicting Muhammad in Danish and French publications, may have been "fueled more by . . . discrimination against Muslim immigrants in Europe than by the [cartoons'] disrespect . . . toward the Prophet."

Given the troubling reality of hateful and discriminatory attitudes, expressions, and actions, which are still too evident throughout our society, I must underscore that I am hardly concluding that these problems have abated. Rather, I am pointing out that the substantial attention and criticism that these problems now receive constitutes a material, positive change, which should reduce the psychic toll of "hate speech" according to the analysis of Delgado, Matsuda, and Lawrence themselves.

INCREASING COUNTERSPEECH BY DISPARAGED PEOPLE

One potential harmful impact of "hate speech" is that it could silence its targets. Although there is merit to this concern, it is allayed by the widespread campus activism in the past several years, as well as the increasing society-wide activism, including the Black Lives Matter, LGBT rights, anti–sexual violence, and pro–immigrants' rights movements. This activism has flourished at the same time that there have been substantial reports of hateful, discriminatory speech, as well as bias crimes, against members of the pertinent groups. In the current environment, the existence of "hate speech" seems to have had a galvanizing impact rather than a silencing one. Shaun Harper, Executive Director of the University of Pennsylvania's Center for the Study of Race and Equity in Education, described this development on campus as "an unmuting of black collegians," commenting that "[t]hey are . . . speaking more loudly" than ever before "about the . . . racism they experience in classrooms and elsewhere."

This encouraging trend of increasing counterspeech seems likely to continue, according to recent surveys of incoming college students; students have indicated that they plan to advocate for social justice not only on campus and during their student days, but also beyond. Because students appear to be motivated by the sense that activism can lead to change, we have reason to hope for an upward spiral: more activism should generate more positive reform, which in turn should galvanize more activism into the future.

CHAPTER SEVEN

. . .

"Hate Speech" Laws Are at Best Ineffective and at Worst Counterproductive

"We must recognize the limits of legislation to combat hate speech."
—Adama Dieng, United Nations Special Adviser on
the Prevention of Genocide

"Legal scholars are dedicated to the theoretical interpretation of
hate speech legislation . . . , but do not examine its actual impact. .
. . [I]t is time to verify whether the theoretical expectations stand
the test of reality."
—Andrea Scheffler, Friedrich-Ebert-Stiftung
(German foundation)

IN THE PRECEDING chapter I explained that constitutionally protected "hate speech" makes only a speculative contribution to the
harms it is feared to cause. In this chapter, I address another reason for rejecting "hate speech" laws: even if such speech did significantly contribute to discrimination, violence, and psychic harms,
censoring it would not significantly reduce the problematic speech
or the feared harms. Moreover, in several important respects, "hate

speech" laws can actually be counterproductive, exacerbating rather than reducing the feared harms. In sum, wholly apart from their constitutional flaws, "hate speech" laws would be bad public policy.

NO CORRELATION WITH REDUCED DISCRIMINATION OR VIOLENCE

As I noted in Chapter 4, many countries with "hate speech" laws have experienced no positive impact in terms of reducing discrimination; it showed that some governments that have enforced criminal "hate speech" laws have brutally discriminated on the bases of race, ethnicity, and religion. Furthermore, professors Louis Greenspan and Cyril Levitt have noted that "[t]he rise of France's National Front party, which under the leadership of Jean-Marie Le Pen was overtly racist, . . . occurred in a country that had supposedly immunized itself" through "hate speech" laws. They concluded further that "'respectable' racists" have gained political power in Germany, even though it "has some of the toughest anti-hate legislation in the world." In 2017, a German journalist observed that "Germans have long argued over whether" this legislation "has worked," citing Germany's "severe problem with right-wing extremist violence," and the strength of the right-wing "Alternative for Germany" party, whose "ideas . . . might be construed as racist," and which received 12.6% of the vote in the September 2017 national elections.

The Rise of Nazism in Germany Despite "Hate Speech" Laws

Given the horrors of the Holocaust, even diehard free speech stalwarts would support "hate speech" laws if they would have averted that atrocity. That is certainly the case for me, as the daughter of a German-born Holocaust survivor, who nearly died at Buchenwald.

That also is true for international human rights champion Aryeh Neier, who escaped from Nazi Germany as a child with his immediate family, while the Nazis slaughtered his extended family. Neier was the ACLU's executive director in 1977–78, when the ACLU successfully defended the First Amendment rights of neo-Nazis to demonstrate in Skokie, Illinois. Because he is a renowned free speech absolutist, readers will be surprised to learn that Neier has said that he would support "hate speech" laws if they would have forestalled Nazism:

> I am unwilling to put anything, even love of free speech, ahead of detestation of the Nazis. . . . I could not bring myself to advocate freedom of speech in Skokie if I did not believe that the chances are best for preventing a repetition of the Holocaust in a society where every incursion on freedom is resisted. Freedom has its risks. Suppression of freedom, I believe, is a sure prescription for disaster.

Proponents of "hate speech" laws assume that the enforcement of such laws might have prevented the spread of Nazi ideology in Germany, but the historical record belies this assumption. Throughout the Nazis' rise to power, there were laws on the books criminalizing hateful, discriminatory speech, which were similar to contemporary "hate speech" laws. As noted by Alan Borovoy, general counsel of the Canadian Civil Liberties Association, when he opposed Canada's current "hate speech" legislation:

> Remarkably, pre-Hitler Germany had laws very much like the Canadian anti-hate law. Moreover, those laws were enforced with some vigour. During the fifteen years before Hitler came to power, there were more than two hundred prosecutions based on anti-Semitic speech. And, in the opinion of the leading Jewish

organization of that era, no more than 10% of the cases were
mishandled by the authorities.

The German "hate speech" laws were enforced even against leading Nazis, some of whom served substantial prison terms. But rather
than suppressing the Nazis' anti-Semitic ideology, these prosecutions helped the Nazis gain attention and support. For example,
journalist Flemming Rose reports that between 1923 and 1933, the
virulently anti-Semitic newspaper *Der Stürmer*, published by Julius
Streicher, "was either confiscated or [its] editors [were] taken to
court on . . . thirty-six occasions." Yet, "[t]he more charges Streicher
faced, the greater became the admiration of his supporters. The
courts became an important platform for Streicher's campaign
against the Jews."

The major problem with Germany's response to rising Nazism
was not that the Nazis enjoyed too much free speech, but that the
Nazis literally got away with murder. In effect, they stole free speech
from everyone else, including anti-Nazis, Jews, and other minorities.
As Aryeh Neier commented in his classic book about the Skokie
case: "The lesson of Germany in the 1920s is that a free society
cannot be . . . maintained if it will not act . . . forcefully to punish
political violence. It is as if no effort had been made in the United
States to punish the murderers of Medgar Evers, Martin Luther
King, Jr. . . . and . . . other victims" of violence during the civil rights
movement.

No Inter-Country Correlation

Based on extensive experience in countries around the world,
Human Rights Watch repeatedly has concluded that suppressing
"hate speech" does not effectively promote equality. In 1992, in
response to the push for campus "hate speech" codes to remedy

discrimination, Human Rights Watch issued a report that endorsed the U.S. opposition to "hate speech" laws, explaining: "[A] careful review of the experience of many other countries . . . has made clear that there is little connection in practice between draconian 'hate speech' laws and the lessening of ethnic and racial violence or tension."

Other experts have reaffirmed this conclusion. In 2013, the European Parliament acknowledged that "hate speech" and bias crimes were increasing in European Union countries despite their strong "hate speech" laws. A 2011 study of "hate speech" laws that was prepared for the UN High Commissioner for Human Rights concluded that "massive . . . criminal regulations" of hateful speech did "not seem to have made a meaningful contribution to reducing racism or . . . discriminatory conduct." Likewise, in his 2016 book, which surveyed the experience of many mature democracies with "hate speech" laws, Oxford University professor Timothy Garton Ash concluded that there is no correlation between the existence of such laws and any reduction in the amount of either hateful speech or discriminatory conduct. France, for example, "which has a relatively high level of hate speech prosecutions," nonetheless experienced "endemic discrimination in its labour market [and] racist . . . [chants] in its football stadiums." This negative assessment was echoed by Joel Dreyfuss, former managing editor of "The Root," a black-oriented website: "In terms of racial progress, France looks more like the U.S. in the 1950s—minus enforced segregation—than America today."

One instructive contrast concerns anti-Semitic expression and violence. In 2013, the European Union Fundamental Rights Agency conducted a survey of European Jews. Seventy-six percent said that anti-Semitism had become worse in their countries within the last five years, despite the prevalence of European "hate speech" laws. Similarly, recent surveys by the Anti-Defamation League showed that France had twice the level of anti-Semitism as the United States, despite France's vigorous enforcement of its strict "hate speech" laws against anti-Semitic expression. The lessons to be drawn from this experience were summarized by Jacob Mchangama, founder and director of Justitia, a Copenhagen-based think tank:

> [I]t is even illegal to advocate the boycotting of Israel [in France]. Yet the confluence of increasingly draconian "hate speech" laws and an increase in anti-Semitic attitudes should give [European] lawmakers pause. . . . [S]uch legislation . . . may have actually increased [anti-Semitism]. Likewise, laws against denying the Holocaust . . . may have even encouraged Holocaust denial by endowing it with a veneer of . . . intellectual martyrdom.

No Intra-Country Correlation

There is no evidence that countries that enact "hate speech" laws experience a decline in the amount of either hateful speech or discriminatory behavior. Of the many illustrations of this non-correlation, I will cite just a few. Britain adopted its first "hate speech" law in 1965. Recalling his own personal experience of racist attacks, as someone who had been born in India, British writer Kenan Malik has observed that the ensuing decade "was probably the most racist in British history," involving not only "'Paki-bashing,' when racist thugs would seek out Asians to beat up," but also "openly racist" public institutions, including "police [and] immigration officials." Focusing on the current European situation, Agnès Callamard, Director of Columbia Global Freedom of Expression, noted in 2015 that although "European governments have produced more laws . . . prohibit[ing] 'Hate Speech' than any other region, with the possible exception of the Middle East," European countries "are ravaged by intolerance and . . . increasing inequality," citing "rising levels of violence and hate, anti-immigrant, anti-Roma and anti-Semitic rhetoric" throughout Europe.

Another study was conducted by two Australian professors, who examined the impact of that country's multiple "hate speech" laws from 1989, when the first such law was enacted, through 2010. The authors concluded that after the laws were enacted, minority communities in Australia continued to experience "high levels of verbal abuse" and in some cases even an increase in such abuse. As one final example, I will cite a research project that tracked "hate speech" in Kenya leading up to its 2013 elections. Kenya had adopted a "hate speech" law in 2008 in an effort to stem the type of rampant intergroup violence that had occurred during the 2007–08 post-election period. Notwithstanding this law, the study concluded that "hate speech," including calls for discriminatory violence, was "still . . . serious [and] extensive."

WHY "HATE SPEECH" LAWS ARE INEFFECTIVE AND SOMETIMES EVEN COUNTERPRODUCTIVE

"Nothing strengthens hate groups more than censoring them, as it turns them into free speech martyrs, feeds their sense of grievance, and forces them to seek out more destructive means of activism. . . . Conversely, as the aftermath of Charlottesville has proved, nothing exposes the evil of such groups, and thus weakens them, like letting them show their true nature."

—Glenn Greenwald, journalist

The lack of correlation between "hate speech" laws and reduced discrimination or violence is not surprising in light of several features of such laws, which make them ineffective in reducing hateful speech and thus in reducing the harms that such speech is feared to cause.

Inevitable Underenforcement

As I discussed in Chapter 4, "hate speech" regulations are invariably unduly vague, so that those charged with enforcing them must make discretionary judgments. As I showed, some such judgments are inevitably overinclusive, but, equally inevitably, many are underinclusive. The underenforcement problem is especially acute in countries that lack longstanding democratic structures or traditions, where powerful political figures routinely engage in speech that violates their countries' "hate speech" laws but are not held legally accountable for doing so. This is true, for example, in Poland, where popular politicians target gays, Jews, Roma, and other ethnic minorities; Hungary, where powerful political groups target Roma and Gypsy minorities; Zimbabwe, where President Robert Mugabe's loyalists target his political opponents; India, where powerful politicians, including Prime Minister Narendra Modi, target marginalized minority castes, religions, and sects; and Rwanda and Kenya, where government officials target ethnic minorities. Likewise, Singaporean LGBT rights activists have complained that "the LGBT community in Singapore . . . experience[s] hate speech . . . in public statements by influential newsmakers, such as politicians or religious leaders," but receives "no . . . protection" under that country's "hate speech" laws. Journalism professor Cherian George has concluded that "hate speech" laws are less effective than "US political culture" in constraining "politicians who indulge in hate speech," with the result that "hate speech appears more flagrant and prevalent in elections in India than in the United States, despite the wider latitude that the First Amendment offers American politicians."

Ironically but predictably, it is precisely in those countries where there is the most discrimination, and the most "hate speech," that authorities are least likely to enforce laws, including "hate speech" laws, designed to prevent or redress such discrimination. This point was stressed in a study of such laws in Latin America by Fordham Law School professor Tanya Hernandez, who concluded:

> Entrusting the enforcement of . . . [a] criminal ["hate speech"] law to public authorities risks having the law undermined by the complacent inaction of public officials who may harbor the same racial bias as the agents of hate speech. This is a particular danger in Latin America where police officers are consistently found to discourage Afro-descendants from filing racial discrimination complaints, and are often the perpetrators of discrimination and violence themselves.

Targeting Only Blatant Expression

"[I]n American society today, the real power commanded by the racist is likely to vary inversely with the vulgarity with which it is expressed. . . . [T]hose who [advocate 'hate speech' laws] invite us to spend more time worrying about speech codes than coded speech."
—Harvard University professor Henry Louis Gates, Jr.

As even proponents of "hate speech" laws recognize, legal sanctions must be limited to only the most blatant discriminatory expression; fundamental free speech principles bar government from suppressing the more subtle—and hence more influential—expression of biased views, which pervades our public discourse. For example, Professor Mari Matsuda has maintained that statements about purported "intellectual differences between the races" should be permitted unless they include "an element of hatred or persecution." As explained in Chapter 4, such limits reduce the overbreadth of "hate speech" laws, but they raise other First Amendment problems. First, these limits render "hate speech" laws ineffective with respect to the expression that is most likely to contribute to the feared harms. This means that the laws suppress constitutionally protected "hate speech"—albeit less such speech than a broader law would suppress—without substantially reducing the feared harms. Even more fundamentally, as the Supreme Court has warned, a law that is significantly "underinclusive," by selectively targeting only some of the speech feared to cause the harms at issue, "raises serious doubts about whether the government is in fact pursuing the interest it invokes, rather than disfavoring a particular speaker or viewpoint." Finally, because such laws censor some constitutionally protected "hate speech," the uncensored expression may inadvertently bear the imprimatur of legitimacy.

Harvard professor Henry Louis Gates, Jr. has stressed the endemic underinclusiveness of "hate speech" laws as one reason why he opposes them. To illustrate the problem, he laid out two hypothetical statements addressed to an incoming African-American student at a prestigious university: one that Gates called a "gutter epithet" and one that he called a "disquisition." Gates's hypothesized gutter epithet was: "Out of my face, jungle bunny." Gates's posited disquisition critiqued the university's affirmative action admissions policy, observing that because "aptitude tests place African Americans . . . below the mean," affirmative action "places . . . underprepared . . . black students in demanding educational environments." "Hate speech" laws would presumably punish Gates's epithet, but not the disquisition. Indeed, I am not aware of any proponent of "hate speech" laws in the United States who would advocate extending them to such general statements about public issues. (As I explained in Chapter 3, the epithet might already be punishable, if in the overall context it constituted a true threat, fighting words, or targeted harassment.) Gates reasons that because the disquisition cannot be punished, punishing the epithet "won't do much good, if any". This is so, he argues, because the disquisition is much more likely to contribute to the feared harms that supposedly warrant "hate speech" laws. Harvard law professor Randall Kennedy likewise criticizes "hate speech" laws for supporting a "vocabulary of indirection," under which "the damaging but polite polemic is protected, while the rude but impotent epithet is not."

"Hate speech" laws leave three options for those inclined to engage in hateful, discriminatory speech, all of which have negative consequences for equality and societal harmony: some such expression will be driven underground; some will be camouflaged in more subtle rhetoric to evade punishment; and some will remain unchanged, or perhaps even ramped up, as the speakers seek the publicity that results from prosecution.

Driving Some Expression Underground

"[A]s my grandmother used to tell me, every time a fool speaks, they are just advertising their own ignorance. Let them talk. If you don't, you just make them a victim, and then they can avoid accountability."
—President Barack Obama, 2016 Howard University commencement address

"If hate speech were made completely illegal, what would happen . . . is the intensification of what we already have, which is a denial of the continued significance . . . of race. . . . [It] would drive racism further underground and allow judges and others more freedom to deny its existence and relevance."
—Ted Shaw, former director-counsel and president, NAACP Legal Defense and Educational Fund

Censorship drives some discriminatory expression underground, with important negative consequences. First, because some people who harbor hateful, discriminatory ideas are deterred from expressing them, we don't realize who they are. We therefore lose the opportunity to dissuade them and to monitor their conduct to ensure it is not discriminatory. Second, we lose the opportunity for people to listen to these ideas and to realize their flaws. Third, those of us who deplore such ideas are deprived of the opportunity to formulate and communicate responses, and everyone else is deprived of the opportunity to hear such exchanges. In the long run, an open airing of discriminatory ideas, and an ensuing debate about them, may well be more effective in curbing them than censorship would be. Fourth, as a 2015 UNESCO report observed: "[H]ate speech is . . . a window into deeply-rooted tensions and inequalities, which . . . do need addressing." "Hate speech" thus has the positive impact of energizing citizens to engage in social justice activism in an effort to address the discrimination and hatred that plague our society. In other words, any short-term benefit of suppressing "hate speech" may be outweighed by the long-term benefit of exposing and challenging it. As the old saying puts it, "Sunlight is the best disinfectant."

To illustrate this last downside of driving constitutionally protected "hate speech" underground, I will cite a coalition of civil rights activists and organizations, which has long raised this very complaint about Facebook's enforcement of its ban on "hate speech": that it has impeded their efforts to raise public concern about and mobilization against hateful speech and conduct. As a private-sector entity, Facebook is not bound by First Amendment standards, but its record in enforcing its "hate speech" rules highlights the inherent problems in enforcing (and drafting) any "hate speech" law. One problem that minority activists cite about Facebook's "hate speech" ban is that it blocks them from sharing "hate speech" that was targeted at them, even when they explain—consistent with Facebook protocols—that they are doing so not to perpetuate racism, but rather "to call [it] out" and to seek emotional, psychological support. In short, when the disparaged people quote the "hate speech" that was targeted at them, it is transformed into counterspeech; but "hate speech" laws operate, paradoxically, to censor such counterspeech.

This adverse impact of suppressing responses to "hate speech" was experienced by Francie Latour, who is black. While she was shopping for groceries in Boston with her two young sons, a white man "leaned toward [them] and, just loudly enough for the boys to hear, unleashed a profanity-laced racist epithet." Latour immediately "vented" on Facebook, but her post was promptly deleted for violating Facebook's "hate speech" ban. She said that Facebook's censorship "felt almost exactly like what happened to my sons writ large. . . . They were left with all that ugliness and hate, and when I tried to share it so that people could see it for what it is, I was shut down."

Let me describe one dramatic example of counterspeech that would not have occurred but for a famous episode of constitutionally protected "hate speech" that government officials and many community members vigorously sought to censor: the 1977–78 Skokie case in which neo-Nazis, represented by the ACLU, won the legal right to demonstrate in that heavily Jewish community, which included many Holocaust survivors. In 2009, Skokie opened its Holocaust Museum and Education Center, which is dedicated to "preserving the legacy of the Holocaust by honoring the memories of those who were lost and by teaching universal lessons that combat hatred, prejudice and indifference." As University of Chicago law professor Geoffrey Stone observed: "Ironically, but exquisitely, it was the Skokie controversy that caused the survivors in Skokie and around the world to recognize that . . . 'despite their desire to leave the past behind, they could no longer remain silent,'" so they created this new institution and "dedicated themselves to 'combating hate with education.'"

Incentivizing More Palatable and Thus More Potent Hateful Speech

"Hate speech" laws induce some speakers with hateful ideas to "sugarcoat" them, with the perverse result that they are more widely circulated and accepted. Based on their study of the "hate speech" laws in six European nations, professors Louis Greenspan and Cyril Levitt concluded that these laws had forced politicians with racist agendas to adopt "carefully worded racist programs," making them "more potent." They drew a telling contrast between the sanitized racist expression in Europe and the American Nazi Party's uncensored speech: "With slogans such as 'Hitler was right—he gassed the Jews,' . . . the [U.S.] racist right could make no headway in the general population."

Increasing Attention and Support

Censoring any material increases an audience's desire to obtain it and disposes the audience to be more receptive to it. This phenomenon is so prevalent that several widely used terms have been coined to describe it, including the "boomerang effect," the "forbidden fruits effect," and the "Streisand effect." The latter refers to singer Barbra Streisand, whose attempt to suppress photographs of her Malibu, California home inadvertently greatly increased public attention to it. Moreover, by casting the silenced speaker as a free speech martyr, censorship also ousts critics from the moral high ground. Not surprisingly, then, many hatemongers welcome "hate speech" laws and prosecutions under them.

In part for these reasons, Canada's federal criminal "hate speech" law rarely has been enforced, and it has strongly been criticized as ineffective and even counterproductive. Consider an early major prosecution under that law, against James Keegstra, a virulently anti-Semitic public school teacher. He was charged under the law in 1984, two years after he had been dismissed from his teaching job because of his anti-Semitic indoctrination of students. The ensuing protracted legal proceedings ultimately resulted, in 1996, in a one-year suspended sentence, one year of probation, and 200 hours of community service. As University of Calgary law professor Peter Bowal summed up the case:

> [Fourteen] years from the time Keegstra was dismissed from his teaching job, after two long trials, three sentences, three hearings in the Supreme Court of Canada and six trials and appeals . . . costing an estimated million dollars, an unrepentant Keegstra was sentenced to the equivalent of a tap on the wrist. . . . Ironically, that public stage granted him 14 more years to publicize his opinions. The extensive media coverage of the cumbersome legal saga may even have garnered Keegstra more sympathy.

Given the lack of "social value . . . realized" from the Keegstra prosecution and conviction, Bowal commented, "This may explain why there have been few successful prosecutions" under Canada's criminal "hate speech" law in the years since.

Another famous example of this pattern is the 1977–78 Skokie controversy. Local officials, supported by local Jewish leaders, initially granted the Nazis' request to march precisely to avoid giving them the publicity they craved. When that decision was reversed, the resulting legal battle predictably won the Nazis prolonged national—and even international—media attention that was probably even more valuable to them than their predictable legal victory. The Nazis would have received far less attention had they simply been allowed to proceed with their planned march of short duration (20–30 minutes), with few participants (their probably exaggerated estimate was 30–50).

The Technological Impossibility of Silencing "Hate Speech"

Given the recent explosion of decentralized communications technologies, including the internet and mobile phones, today it is practically impossible to block any type of expression completely. In 2010, when then-President Obama explained to the UN General Assembly why the United States opposes censoring even hateful speech that might lead to violence (except in the rare situation when the emergency test is satisfied), he pointed out, among other reasons, that "when anyone with a cell phone can spread offensive views around the world with the click of a button, the notion that we can control the flow of information is obsolete."

In fact, even after online hatemongers have been imprisoned under "hate speech" laws, their websites remain active. For example, Ernst Zundel, a purveyor of neo-Nazi propaganda, was prosecuted and convicted for engaging in "hate speech" in both Canada and Germany in litigation that dragged out for eleven years, from 1996 to 2007. But as one expert noted in 2010, "Even now, Zundel's website is still running and regularly updated with his 'letters from prison' despite his incarceration."

Enforcement Frustrations

As illustrated by the Canadian *Keegstra* case, an additional drawback of "hate speech" laws from the perspective of the people the speech disparages is that their eventual remedy, and the perpetrator's eventual penalty, if any, often comes too late, and at too high a transaction cost, to afford meaningful relief. The most thorough study of the enforcement problems in these cases was undertaken by Australian professors Katharine Gelber and Luke McNamara, who reviewed the enforcement of their country's "hate speech" laws. Because the Australian laws are typical, there is no reason to believe that the problems Gelber and McNamara documented are in any way out of the ordinary. They concluded that "pursuing a remedy" under Australia's "hate speech" laws is "arduous, stressful, time-consuming, and possibly expensive." Individuals who were targets of such speech, as well as their lawyers and the organizations that supported them, consistently complained that "you might win in the end, but it's going to take so much out of you." Too often, the complainants end up winning what they dismiss as merely "a pyrrhic victory."

HOW EFFECTIVE ARE "HATE SPEECH" LAWS AT REDUCING . . .

. . . *Intergroup Hostility?*

"[Rwanda's "hate speech"] laws have . . . become a tool that fuels further conflict instead of preventing it."
—Andrea Scheffler, author of case study about these laws

"[T]he logging of racist incidents in British schools had the perverse effect of racializing children's perception of each other."
—Oxford University professor Timothy Garton Ash

Far from reducing intergroup violence, hostility, and tensions, "hate speech" laws often tend to fuel them. This problem is so prevalent that communications scholar Cherian George, who has studied these laws in various countries, coined a term to describe it: "hate spin." Politicians "spin" expression by rival groups as "hate speech," bringing charges under their countries' laws, thereby stirring up hostilities, to their political advantage.

Even in developed democracies, enforcement of "hate speech" laws is likely to increase, not decrease, intergroup tensions. Experience teaches that the most effective way to reduce or resolve intergroup conflicts is through cooperative, conciliatory approaches, rather than through "lawfare." The recent explosion of "hate speech" charges has escalated conflicts. People who make such charges convey their strong negative feelings about the speaker's views, essentially saying, "I hate your ideas," and they simultaneously accuse the speaker of being animated by strong negative feelings. Sometimes, though, such expression reflects only ignorance or insensitivity. As psychological experts confirm, assailing speakers who lack malign motives as having engaged in "hate speech" is hardly the most constructive way to persuade them to use more sensitive language in the future. Even for speakers who do harbor hateful attitudes, evidence shows that subjecting them to adversary legal proceedings is not the optimal strategy for inducing positive changes in attitudes or behavior.

A related downside of "hate speech" laws is that they curb the sort of intergroup dialogue about bias that experts consider a precondition for reducing intergroup hatred and discrimination. As Pierre Bierre of Stanford University's Neuropsychology Laboratory has observed, "[T]he first step to resolve conflicts is to get people to open up and share unedited gut feelings . . . , and the second step is to remove the listening blocks that prevent the other side from hearing those feelings." "Hate speech" laws, in contrast, have a chilling impact on both open expression and open-minded listening.

. . . Retaliatory Violence?

> "[I]n a liberal democracy, laws protect those who offend from [being] threat[ened], not those who threaten from being offended."
> —Petition to Danish Parliament

Another potential harm to which constitutionally protected "hate speech" is said to contribute is retaliatory violence against the speaker or the speaker's allies by those who despise the message. If government capitulated to such threats of retaliatory violence by suppressing the speech, that would only encourage further threats and violence rather than curbing them. This was a recurrent theme throughout the civil rights movement, when courts refused to halt speeches and demonstrations by civil rights advocates because of threatened and even actual violence by opponents of their cause.

In 2012, then-President Barack Obama flagged this concern (among others) in explaining to the UN General Assembly why the United States did not censor the anti-Islamic video that was then believed to have spurred the murderous attacks on the U.S. Embassy in Benghazi, Libya: "There are no words that excuse the killing of innocents. . . . In this modern world with modern technologies, for us to respond in that way to hateful speech empowers any individual who engages in such speech to create chaos around the world. We empower the worst of us if that's how we respond."

. . . Psychic or Emotional Harm?

It might seem self-evident that shielding people from speech that could have negative psychic impacts would be positive for their mental health. But some experts maintain that, at least in some circumstances, people's mental health is actually undermined by shielding them from speech to which they have negative psychic reactions, including constitutionally protected "hate speech." In a 2015 article, NYU psychology professor Jonathan Haidt and Greg Lukianoff, the president of FIRE (Foundation for Individual Rights in Education), summarized the pertinent psychological literature and concluded: "A campus culture devoted to policing speech and punishing speakers . . . may be teaching students to think pathologically," causing depression and anxiety. They recommend that, to better protect students' psychic well-being, colleges and universities should abandon rather than enforce restrictive speech codes. As Northeastern University psychology professor Lisa Feldman Barrett wrote in 2017, while "chronic" stress can cause physical illness, shorter-term stress, including the stress that results from hearing "hate speech," actually can be beneficial:

> Offensiveness is not bad for your body and brain. Your nervous system evolved to withstand periodic bouts of stress, such

as fleeing from a tiger . . . or encountering an odious idea. . . .
When you're forced to engage a position you strongly disagree
with . . . [it] feels unpleasant, but it's a good kind of stress—temporary and not harmful to your body—and you reap the longer-
term benefits of learning.

Haidt and Lukianoff add that this "good kind of stress" at least
"sometimes makes an individual stronger and more resilient,"
explaining that "[t]he next time that person faces a similar situation,
she'll experience a milder stress response because . . . her coping
repertoire has grown."

Major studies by researchers at Harvard and at the University of
Wisconsin both have shown that our perceptions of whether stress
is positive or negative can make a big difference in its actual psychological and physiological impact on us. In light of these findings, in
her book, *The Upside of Stress: Why Stress Is Good for You, and How to
Get Good at It*, Stanford psychologist Kelly McGonigal has championed "rethinking stress" to "make [it] your friend." Consistent with
this research, some psychologists maintain that we should educate
students and others to shift their perceptions of hateful speech and
other speech they find objectionable. For example, psychologist
Pamela Paresky writes:

High levels of *perceived* stress are associated with [adverse physiological impacts]. . . . If one person tells herself that listening to
a speaker is going to be intolerable and harmful, . . . the experience will be more stressful for her than . . . for the person who
tells herself it will be . . . an opportunity to defeat a bad idea.
[Moreover, if] we believe that stress causes harm, we may in fact
suffer more harm from stress, while if we believe that stress is
enhancing, we can experience increases in anabolic ("growth")
hormones.

The psychology professors I have quoted above agree in principle on two important points: that chronic stress can cause physical harm, but that facing and overcoming short-term stress can be a positive experience for our mental and physical health. There is some disagreement, though, about how these principles play out in the context of "hate speech" on campus. Feldman Barrett maintains that it is reasonable "not to allow a . . . hatemonger like Milo Yiannopoulos to speak" on campus because "[h]e is part of . . . a campaign of abuse," which makes the campus a "harsh environment," in which students "spend a lot of time worrying about [their] safety." In contrast, Haidt and Paresky maintain that any such reaction to the campus environment results in large part from students' perceptions, so that the most effective intervention is not to shield students from distressing speakers and ideas, but rather to make students more resilient and to alter their perceptions, including their perceptions of their own resilience. In fact, many students and others familiar with the campus environment do not share the perception that it is generally "harsh."

I do not purport to weigh in on one side or the other of these debates among psychological experts. Rather, I simply call attention to the fact that some experts reject the seemingly "obvious" conclusion that reducing exposure to "hate speech" would effectively reduce any associated psychic or emotional harms.

WOULD "HATE SPEECH" LAWS HAVE A POSITIVE SYMBOLIC VALUE?

Given the dearth of evidence that "hate speech" laws actually promote equality, societal harmony, or psychic well-being, it is not surprising that the laws' proponents often maintain that a primary benefit of such laws lies in their "symbolic" value, by expressing society's commitment to these goals. These claims cannot be either substantiated or refuted. Weighing against them, though, are several negative aspects of the symbolism associated with "hate speech" laws.

First, these laws symbolize not only society's commitment to the stated goals, but also society's lack of confidence in freedom of speech and democracy. In opposing "hate speech" laws, Harvard professor Henry Louis Gates, Jr. has stressed this point:

> [O]nce we have admitted that the regulation of racist speech is, in part or whole, a symbolic act, we must register the force of the other symbolic considerations that may come into play. The controversy over flag burning is a good illustration. . . . Perhaps safeguarding the flag symbolized something nice, but for many of us, safeguarding our freedom to burn the flag symbolized something nicer.

Second, marginalized groups who are the intended beneficiaries of "hate speech" laws may well feel that society is offering them mere symbolic or token gestures, at the cost of measures that are actually effective. Gates has critiqued the symbolism defense of "hate speech" laws for this reason also, stating: "Speech codes . . . let a group of people say, 'This symbolizes that we . . . are not the sort of community where we would tolerate someone saying . . . 'rigger' [*sic*]. Well, big deal." During a 2015 interview, then-President Obama made a similar point: "Racism, we are not cured of it. And it's not just a matter of it not being polite to say 'nigger' in public."

Third, a society's expressions of commitment to equality, societal harmony, and psychic well-being are likely to carry more meaningful symbolic weight if undertaken voluntarily by individual members of the community and government officials, and in response to specific situations. Voluntary counterspeech by community members and leaders, specifically responding to particular instances of hateful, discriminatory speech, would surely be more meaningful to the disparaged people than a general official statement condemning constitutionally protected "hate speech" in the abstract. Of course, this is not an either–or choice, and members of our society could pursue such voluntary counterspeech efforts as a complement to "hate speech" laws. As a practical matter, though, the laws apparently have decreased community members' incentives to do so in at least some situations. Accordingly, multiple European human rights agencies recently have urged increasing reliance on counterspeech and other non-censorial countermeasures, as Chapter 1 discussed.

THE COSTS OF "HATE SPEECH" LAWS OUTWEIGH
THEIR BENEFITS

"There is a compelling case that the advantages of hate speech laws, as they have actually worked over the last half century, are outweighed by the disadvantages."
—Oxford University professor Timothy Garton Ash

The case for censoring constitutionally protected "hate speech" is often based largely on reciting the potential harms to which such speech is feared to contribute, with no rigorous analysis of other factors that we logically must consider in evaluating whether such laws are warranted. As this chapter has shown, though, "hate speech" laws do not effectively suppress constitutionally protected "hate speech" or its feared harmful impact, and might even aggravate at least some feared harms. Moreover, as we have seen, such laws would gravely damage core principles that secure freedom of speech, equality, and democracy. Finally, as the next chapter shows, experts concur that non-censorial alternative measures, including counterspeech, are "much more" effective than "hate speech" laws in reducing both the incidence and potential harmful impact of constitutionally protected "hate speech."

CHAPTER EIGHT

Non-censorial Methods Effectively Curb the Potential Harms of Constitutionally Protected "Hate Speech"

In 2015, the European Commission against Racism and Intolerance (ECRI) issued a report strongly urging European nations to pursue non-censorial responses to "hate speech." This is especially noteworthy because in recent decades many European nations have enacted "hate speech" laws with the encouragement of regional bodies, including ECRI. But, as a result of its monitoring of the efforts of European nations to curb "hate speech" and discrimination, ECRI has concluded that alternative, non-censorial measures are *"much more likely"* than laws forbidding "hate speech" "to prove effective in ultimately eradicating" "hate speech" and its potential harmful effects. In this chapter, I discuss some important examples of such alternative measures.

COUNTERSPEECH

The term "counterspeech" encompasses any speech that counters a message with which one disagrees. Justice Brandeis's historic 1927 concurring opinion in *Whitney v. California*, which rejected the majority's bad tendency doctrine and endorsed the emergency test, celebrated counterspeech as the appropriate alternative to censorship: "The fitting remedy for evil counsels is good ones. . . . If there be time to expose through discussion the falsehood and fallacies, to avert the evil by the processes of education, the remedy to be applied is more speech, not enforced silence." In the half-century since the Supreme Court unanimously embraced Brandeis's approach, it has vigorously endorsed this "more speech" "remedy" for an expanding range of expression whose messages are disfavored, disturbing, or feared.

In the context of "hate speech," counterspeech comprises a potentially broad range of expression, including speech that directly refutes the ideas the "hate speech" conveys; broader, proactive educational initiatives; and expressions of remorse by discriminatory speakers. I will first discuss evidence that counterspeech can be effective in checking the potentially harmful effects of "hate speech," and I will then offer some specific examples of counterspeech strategies.

THE EFFECTIVENESS OF COUNTERSPEECH

"[E]xtremist speech . . . can be more effectively undermined by adding favorable messages . . . than by deleting extremist content."
—2016 Report about Counterspeech on Twitter

The internet's unparalleled facilitation of instantaneous, worldwide communication is a double-edged sword in terms of hateful speech. The internet not only makes it easier than ever to convey hateful messages; it also makes it easier than ever to rebut them. What's more, the internet makes it easier to measure the extent and impact of counterspeech. Although the field is still young, there have been promising online counterspeech initiatives and studies of their efficacy. For example:

- Google has added to its website a disclaimer about sites containing hateful messages. If any such site shows up prominently in response to a search request, the user will see an explanation of how search results are ranked, as well as an apology, to dispel any impression that Google endorses such messages.
- YouTube has developed videos to counter hateful messages.
- Facebook has created tools that enable users to privately notify authors of content they find objectionable before formally asking Facebook to remove it.
- Facebook engaged the public policy organization Demos to undertake research about the extent to which counterspeech is produced and shared on Facebook. Demos's initial report, issued in 2015, found that hateful online speech is "often met with disagreement, derision, and counter-campaigns," and that this "crowd-sourced response" has significant advantages over suppression: "[I]t is faster, more flexible and responsive, [and] capable of dealing with [problematic expression] from anywhere and in any language." Some Facebook users actively search out "hate speech" for the express purpose of challenging it. Some counterspeech is shared publicly, and some is conveyed via private communications with the speaker. The report concluded that some types of content and format were especially effective

at countering "hate speech," especially photos and videos, "constructive" comments, and comments about specific policy issues.

In 2016, a report was issued about counterspeech on Twitter, coauthored by a group of scholars from the United States and Canada. The report, which included the first review of the "small body" of existing research about online counterspeech, concluded that hateful and other "extremist" speech was most effectively "undermined" by counterspeech rather than by removing it. One reason for this conclusion is that "content is likely to reappear elsewhere on the Internet after it has been deleted." Echoing the Demos report about Facebook, the Twitter report concluded that images are more persuasive than text alone, and that humor, including satire, is especially powerful. The report indicated that by combining these two approaches, humor and images, "people who do not share a language" can effectively "counterspeak together, often in large numbers and across cultural and national boundaries." Among the examples offered by the report was the following:

> Dani Alves, a [black] Brazilian soccer player, was subjected to a humiliating racist gesture when a spectator threw a banana at him on the field. . . . Another player . . . quickly posted an image of himself eating a banana, on the hashtag #Somostodosmacacos, meaning "we are all monkeys." That hashtag . . . spread quickly. . . . [T]housands of people posted banana-eating selfies in spontaneous support.

Impressively, the Twitter report noted situations in which counterspeech was able to accomplish "lasting change in beliefs" even when the speaker seemed "firmly committed . . . to hateful ideology" and "to declaring it publicly." The report identified the strategies that were successful in these situations, including the use of an empathic or kind tone in response to the speaker rather than targeting the speaker as hateful or racist (although identifying the speech as such). Here is the report's description of an especially inspiring instance of effective counterspeech:

> Megan Phelps-Roper . . . was fully convinced of the extreme homophobic tenets of the Westboro Baptist Church, which her grandfather Fred Phelps founded and in which she was raised— until she started a Twitter account to spread the views of the church. On Twitter she encountered people who challenged her views. . . . Extended conversations with two of them . . . completely changed Phelps-Roper's views, by her own account. She ended up leaving the church.

Paradoxically, in some circumstances the most effective form of counterspeech can be silence. By deliberately choosing to ignore provocative, hateful speakers, silence can powerfully convey implicit messages of disdain, while at the same time denying hateful speakers the attention they seek and often get from sparking controversy. Those engaged in counterspeech should be careful not to act in ways that are ultimately counterproductive, including efforts to silence hateful speakers through aggressive counter-demonstrations. Although such tactics might seem morally justified, they almost always backfire.

The Southern Poverty Law Center (SPLC), for example, which "is dedicated to fighting hate and bigotry," strongly opposes such counter-protests on strategic grounds. In 2017, it issued a guide for students about how to curb the alt-right's increasing campus recruitment efforts. The guide recommends a number of steps, including seeking to persuade the group that invited the alt-right speaker to campus to withdraw its invitation, speaking out peacefully against the event, and meeting with campus groups that the alt-right targets, such as minority student groups, to provide mutual support. The first and foremost strategy that the guide recommends, though, is "above all, avoid confrontation with the alt-right speaker and supporters":

> The alt-right thrives on hostility, and hate feeds on crowds. Video footage of an altercation will only provide cover for the speaker, who can claim to be a victim. As hard as it may be to resist yelling at alt-right speakers, do not confront them. Do not debate them. . . . As this publication makes clear, there are many other ways to challenge [their] beliefs.

Rather than aggressively confronting hateful speakers in counter-demonstrations, the SPLC recommends holding "an alternative event—away from the alt-right event—to highlight your campus' commitment to inclusion and our nation's democratic values." Examples of such nonconfrontational events include "a festival for diversity and tolerance," including music and other entertainment as well as speakers, and "hosting a conference, vigil or forum."

A variation on the latter approaches is what the *New York Times* labeled "humorous subversion," in a 2017 article describing how anti-Nazi Germans have turned an annual neo-Nazi march in one town into an "involuntary walkathon":

> For every meter the neo-Nazis marched, local residents and businesses pledged to donate 10 euros . . . to a program that helps people leave right-wing extremist groups.
>
> They turned the march into a mock sporting event. Someone stenciled onto the street "start," . . . and a finish line, as if it were a race. . . . A sign at the end of the route thanked the marchers for their contribution to the anti-Nazi cause—€10,000.

This subversive humor strategy also has been deployed elsewhere, including in Charlotte, North Carolina, where counterprotestors at a 2012 "white power" march wore clown costumes, held signs reading "wife power," and tossed "white flour." As the *Times* commented: "By undercutting the gravitas white supremacists are trying to accrue, humorous counterprotests may blunt the events' usefulness for recruitment." While "[b]rawling with bandanna-clad antifas may seem romantic to some disaffected young men," serving as the target of ridicule should hardly be a lure.

Experts stress that the foregoing types of tactics have historically been proven more effective than militant confrontation. In their 2011 book *Why Civil Resistance Works*, Erica Chenowith and Maria Stephan concluded that "in over 320 conflicts between 1900 and 2006, nonviolent resistance was more than twice as effective as violent resistance in achieving change."

EMPOWERING DISPARAGED PEOPLE

"I got tough talk for my liberal colleagues on . . . campuses. . . . I don't want you to be safe, ideologically. I don't want you to be safe, emotionally. I want you to be strong. . . . I want you to be deeply aggrieved and offended and upset, and then to learn how to speak back. Because that is what we need from you."
—Van Jones, commentator and social justice activist

"I believe deeply that minority group members who are discriminated against . . . have the . . . responsibility [to] speak on their own behalf."
—Theodore Shaw, former director-counsel and president, NAACP Legal Defense and Educational Fund

"We have to teach [our young people] how to deal with adversarial situations. They have to learn how to survive with offensive speech they find wounding and hurtful."
—Gwen Thomas, civil rights activist

"The . . . protection [of a "hate speech" law] incapacitates. . . . To . . . be told that white folks have the moral character to shrug off insults, and that I do not. . . . That is . . . the most racist statement of all!"
—Conservative political activist Alan Keyes

While all of the activists quoted above are African American, they are ideologically diverse, spanning the left–right spectrum. They all agree, though, that "hate speech" laws that aim to promote equal rights in fact do the opposite, through paternalism and protection-ism. Rather than relying on "hate speech" laws to suppress hate-ful speech, these activists urge those who are disparaged by such expression to confront it directly. Admittedly, this is often "easier said than done," for as the proponents of "hate speech" laws argue, such speech can have both the intent and the effect of silencing those it disparages. This effect can be especially acute in the case of individually targeted "hate speech." Indeed, I vividly recall the first time I was personally the target of a vicious anti-Semitic slur. Although I was a well-educated young adult, I was nonetheless stunned into silence.

As I have noted in prior chapters, we have seen increasing social justice advocacy nationwide in recent years, with members of minor-ity groups actively leading and engaging in such efforts. Surveys indicate that this trend promises to continue. It is essential for the well-being of both individuals and society that we encourage and facilitate such counterspeech rather than adopting the disempower-ing, anti-democratic censorial approach. As the psychologist Pamela Paresky has observed about the campus situation:

Professors and administrators . . . can compassionately encour-age students to overcome their discomfort about objectionable ideas, or they can . . . convince them they need protection from words that cause them "injury." The latter, however, is a recipe for misery. It only serves to create "victims" (or, at best, "survivors"), rather than joyful and effective human beings who not only thrive but are able to make a difference in the world.

As I have acknowledged, in some instances the adverse psychic and emotional impact of "hate speech" might be so incapacitating for some people that they are unable to engage in effective counterspeech, at least in the moment, and other people who are exposed to such speech might lack the education or access to means of communication that would make their counterspeech effective. These are serious concerns, which can and must be addressed through a range of measures, including proactive counseling and training about engaging constructively with "hate speech," education about utilizing social media and other communications vehicles for drawing attention and responding to "hate speech," and providing access to helpful technology, organizations, and other resources. Fortunately, there is a rapidly expanding treasure trove of easily accessible online resources.

A related problem with advocating counterspeech by those who are targeted by "hate speech"—as the above-quoted African-American activists do—is that it is arguably unfair to expect the targeted persons to shoulder this burden; in effect, this imposes on the victims of the speech at least some of the responsibility to rectify its potential harms. While this is a significant issue, there are countervailing considerations. First, such individuals of course have no *duty* to engage in counterspeech. Second, others in our society who are committed to equality and individual dignity have a moral responsibility to condemn "hate speech" and to express support for people whom it targets. Third, the time, effort, and energy that disparaged people expend to engage in counterspeech can be viewed as a sound investment that will yield benefits for them personally, as well as for all concerned. Barack Obama has repeatedly articulated this view.

Having exhorted minority students to engage in counterspeech in response to racist speech, he acknowledged that this "may not seem fair, but ... if you want to make life fair, then you've got to start with the world as it is." As he told the 2017 Howard University graduating class in his commencement address: "[Y]ou have the responsibility to speak up in the face of injustice. . . . And you might as well start practicing now, because . . . you will have to deal with ignorance, hatred, racism ... at every stage of your life."

I consider the responsibility to raise our voices against hateful speech to be especially incumbent on those of us who oppose censorship and urge counterspeech as the right alternative. The ACLU's longstanding position on "hate speech" and other speech that conveys messages inconsistent with civil liberties reflects this stance. The ACLU not only opposes censorship of anti–civil liberties messages; it furthermore urges civil libertarians to raise their voices against those messages. This perspective also has been endorsed by Ted Shaw, former head of the NAACP Legal Defense and Educational Fund, who observed: "[I]f we [in our legal system] tolerate hate speech, then the social compact ought to be that when people hear hate speech ... they ... condemn it; no matter to whom it's directed. . . . [W]henever you see it, as uncomfortable as it may be, you have to condemn it, *on the spot, right there.*"

One excellent example of the effective, empowering use of counterspeech on the part of disparaged people comes from Arizona State University (ASU) in Tempe, Arizona. Under the leadership of an ASU law professor, Charles Calleros, the faculty and administration rejected a "hate speech" code, instead endorsing an educational or counterspeech response to such speech. As a Latino, and thus a member of a minority group himself, Calleros has written about the positive impact of ASU's non-censorial approach, explaining how it has been empowering for would-be "victims" of "hate speech."

Here is Calleros's description of the first "hate speech" incident under ASU's "more speech" policy:

> [F]our black women students . . . were understandably outraged when they noticed a racially degrading poster near the residence of a friend they were visiting in Cholla, a campus dormitory. . . . [They] knocked on the door that displayed the racist poster and expressed their outrage . . . to the occupant who answered. . . . He agreed that the poster was inappropriate [and] removed it. . . . [T]he four students then met with the staff director of Cholla [who] set up a [meeting] for all members of Cholla. . . . [A] capacity crowd showed up. . . . All seemed to accept the challenging conclusion that the poster was protected by the First Amendment, and I regard what followed as a model . . . response.
>
> First, the black women who discovered the poster explained . . . why the poster hurt them deeply. . . . The Anglo-American students assured the black women that they did not share the stereotypes reflected in the poster, yet all agreed that they would benefit from learning more about other cultures. The group reached a consensus that they would support ASU's Black History events and would work toward developing multicultural programming at Cholla. The four women who led the discussion expressed their desire to meet with the residents of the offending dormitory room to exchange views and to educate them about their feelings and about the danger of stereotyping. . . .
>
> The entire University community then poured its energy into . . . constructive action and dialogue. . . . Students organized an open forum. The message was this: at most, a few individuals on campus think that the racist poster is humorous; in contrast, a great number of demonstrators represent the more prevalent campus view that degrading racial stereotypes are destructive.

Such a message is infinitely more effective than disciplining the students who displayed the racist poster.

One of the student leaders of the constructive university-wide response was Rossie Turman, who was then chairman of ASU's African-American Coalition. He stated:

> When you get a chance to swing at racism, and you do, you feel more confident about doing it the next time. It was a personal feeling of empowerment, that I don't have to take that kind of stupidity. . . . The sickest thing would have been if the racists had been kicked out, the university sued, and people were forced to defend these folks. It would have been a momentary victory, but we would have lost the war.

EDUCATION

> "No one is born hating another person because of the color of his skin or his background or his religion. . . . People must learn to hate, and if they can learn to hate, they can be taught to love."
> —Nelson Mandela

> "Over a lifetime spent fighting on the battlefield of civil rights, I've seen how movies can be one of the most effective weapons in our arsenal. As a young man, I marveled at Sidney Poitier challenging prejudice in 'Guess Who's Coming to Dinner?' and giving as good as he got in 'In the Heat of the Night.' When we see injustice from another perspective on the screen, it makes us more aware of real-life injustices around us."
> —Vernon E. Jordan, Jr., civil rights activist

Education is a vital form of counterspeech. One key educational strategy is to convey accurate, positive information about traditionally marginalized groups. This proactive approach should complement other responses to specific instances of "hate speech." It can be pursued in myriad ways, including through the school system, mass media, social media, and entertainment. Social science studies have shown that positive media depictions reduce prejudice and promote a more tolerant and integrated society. These studies parallel the famous "intergroup contact theory" that psychologist Gordon Allport pioneered in the mid-twentieth century about the positive impact of actual contact with people from other groups. In 1956, sociology professors Donald Horton and Richard Wohl coined the term "para-social interaction" to refer to the illusion of face-to-face relationships that audience members sensed with mass media characters. Since then, social scientists have continued to document that media exposure generates the same prejudice-reducing impact as real-world intergroup contact.

Initiatives to counter discrimination through media depictions began in the immediate aftermath of the Holocaust. In 1947, for example, Hollywood released two films that exposed the anti-Semitism that was still pervasive in North America: *Gentleman's Agreement* and *Crossfire*. Although both films were artistically acclaimed, they were controversial—and almost not made—because of the very anti-Semitism they were created to counteract. Today's ongoing controversies about "#Oscarsowhite" and "#Emmysowhite" make clear that, for all the progress we have made in the entertainment industry since 1947, much remains to be done.

It is especially important to provide positive role models for young people. Again, we are making progress, but must make more. To cite just one example, the Cooperative Children's Book Center (CCBC) at the University of Wisconsin has been publicizing and seeking to close the "diversity gap" in children's literature. Its 2014 statistics revealed that in the prior 21 years, only 10% of children's books featured children of color, with girls of color especially underrepresented. In 2014, that number had increased to 14%, perhaps in part due to CCBC's efforts.

Many other educational initiatives can curb the potential negative effects of "hate speech." For members of minority groups who are disparaged by "hate speech," it is especially important to develop the skills and outlooks that can help them to avert or minimize the potentially adverse psychic and emotional impact of such speech, and to refute its message. Some psychologists endorse teaching college students and others general cognitive-behavioral therapy techniques for reducing anxiety or other negative reactions that might result from stressful situations, including exposure to "hate speech." Psychologists also endorse educational approaches for developing people's "resilience" in the face of such situations—their ability to maintain their sense of self-esteem and to carry on effectively with their work and personal activities.

As for speakers who purvey hateful messages, it is important for them to understand the potentially harmful effects of their speech on themselves as well as others. The organizations that engage in this kind of education include the Chicago-based Life After Hate, founded in 2009 by former members of violent, far-right white power groups. It provides emotional support to current members of such groups who seek to leave them; assists family members who seek to persuade a loved one to consider alternative viewpoints; and tries to dissuade potential recruits from joining such groups.

Even beyond all of this, there are important lessons for us to learn about ourselves and our society. Colleges and universities, for example, have increasingly offered courses and programs designed to explore the existence of implicit or unconscious biases and steps to overcome them; the discrimination and violence that adversely affect many minority groups in our society; the phenomenon of "white privilege"; the psychic, dignitary, and other harms to which "hate speech" may contribute; language that is inadvertently insensitive and offensive; how to respond to discriminatory or other negative messages about ourselves and groups to which we belong; critical listening and learning skills, so that we don't unthinkingly accept information or ideas to which we are exposed; and how counterspeech can help prevent or redress the potential harms of "hate speech."

These issues are, of course, complex and controverted, and should be studied in a manner that is consistent with academic freedom principles. The goal is to learn how to think critically about these issues, not to be "brainwashed." Students should be free— indeed, encouraged—to raise differing perspectives and to engage in vigorous discussion and debate. That, after all, is the essence of education.

These topics should be explored not only in formal educational settings, but also by all members of our society, including through the abundant pertinent online materials. As James Madison observed, "the . . . diffusion of knowledge is the only guardian of true liberty," and it is an equally essential underpinning of our democracy.

DEVELOPING THICKER AND THINNER SKIN

"No one can make you feel inferior without your consent."
—Eleanor Roosevelt

"A speaker's racial epithet . . . harms the hearer only through [the hearer's] understanding of the message. . . . The harm occurs . . . only to the extent that the hearer (mentally) responds one way rather than another, for example, as a victim rather than as a critic of the speaker."
—Professor C. Edwin Baker

I would like to comment briefly on two of the above-mentioned educational strategies for responding to "hate speech": learning how to become less sensitive to "hate speech" that targets us, and learning how to become more sensitive to "hate speech" that targets others. For our own well-being, we should develop relatively thick skins, so that our sense of self-confidence is not threatened by hateful words. This is how I understand that old nursery rhyme, "Sticks and stones may break my bones, but words will never hurt me." It is not a statement of fact; all of us have been hurt by words in myriad ways. Not only have they hurt our feelings, but they have also broken our hearts, wounded our pride, and contributed to countless other negative emotions, sometimes with physical manifestations.

Given the indisputable power of words to hurt us, the old nursery rhyme is not a descriptive statement about the inability of words to hurt, but an exhortation, encouraging us to respond to words in a way that empowers us and disempowers those who seek to hurt us. This implicit meaning becomes explicit through the insertion of just two words: "Sticks and stones may break my bones, but words [I] will never [let] hurt me." This is precisely the point of Eleanor Roosevelt's epigram above.

To be sure, some of us are less able than others to withstand the hurtful impact of particular wounding words, including "hate speech." A member of a marginalized minority group will likely find it harder than others to face down discriminatory words with the attitude that they "will never hurt me." Moreover, each of us has our own unique degree of (in)sensitivity to hurtful words; we range across the spectrum from the most thin-skinned to the most thick-skinned. But no matter who we are as individuals, and no matter to which societal groups we belong, we can—and must—increase our capacity to resist the hurtful potential of hateful, discriminatory words that target us, while also becoming more sensitive to such words that target others. In short, *we should develop thicker skin on behalf of ourselves and thinner skin on behalf of others.*

All of this is, of course, "easier said than done." Nonetheless, behavioral psychologists and other experts attest to having taught their patients methods for resisting, reducing, and rebounding from the adverse effects that they would otherwise experience in stressful situations, including exposure to "hate speech." Likewise, experts have developed educational techniques for increasing our empathy for others.

Apologies

> "'I'm sorry' are the two most healing words in the English language."
> —Psychologist Harriet Lerner

A specific "more speech" measure that experts have hailed as mutually beneficial, both for those who engage in "hate speech" and for those whom they disparage, is a refreshingly simple one: sincere apology. Proponents of "hate speech" laws stress that the targeted speech can contribute to adverse psychological and physiological effects. It therefore should not be surprising that healing words, in the form of sincere apologies, can have positive psychological and physiological benefits. Psychotherapist Beverly Engel cites research showing that "receiving an apology has a noticeable positive physical effect on the body. . . . [I]t actually affects the bodily functions of the person receiving it—blood pressure decreases, heart rate slows and breathing becomes steadier." An apology also benefits the person who makes it. Psychologist Harriet Lerner writes:

> The courage to apologize . . . is not just a gift to the injured person, who can then feel . . . released from . . . corrosive anger. It's also a gift to [the apologizer's] own health, bestowing

self-respect . . . [and] an ability to take a clear-eyed look at how our behavior affects others and to assume responsibility for acting at another person's expense.

Experts warn, however, that the benefits of sincere apologies do not flow if they are coerced. According to Engel, an apology that you make "because someone else tells you it is the right thing to do" will lack healing power. This is yet another reason why we should address discriminatory speech through a constructive educational approach rather than an adversarial, punitive one.

The actual experience under "hate speech" laws confirms the psychologists' teachings. Two scholars concluded that one reason why Australia's "hate speech" laws are counterproductive is that they undermine the constructive remedy that a sincere apology can afford. Professors Katharine Gelber and Luke McNamara reported that people who are disparaged by hateful, discriminatory speech initially "tend to seek" only "genuine apologies." However, when the protracted legal proceedings finally do culminate with a court-ordered apology, this "frustrates complainants who seek a genuine acknowledgement of wrong-doing."

Counterspeech by Government and Campus Officials

Social scientists have confirmed that counterspeech by leaders in the pertinent community is especially persuasive in rebutting hateful speech—and, hence, in countering its potential harmful effects. Government officials may engage in counterspeech as long as their counterspeech does not, in practical effect, have such a deterrent effect on the ideas at issue as to become the functional equivalent of censorship. If it is difficult to draw the line between censuring and censoring in a specific situation, the official should refrain from comment.

To reduce the danger of *de facto* suppression, officials who are engaging in counterspeech should stress that they are not seeking to punish the speaker. A fine model of this approach was President Obama's 2012 speech to the UN General Assembly shortly after the terrorist attacks on the U.S. embassy in Benghazi, Libya. At the time, it was believed that these attacks had been instigated by an anti-Muslim video that recently had been posted to YouTube. Obama strongly deplored the video's viewpoint but he also strongly defended the free speech rights of its creators and distributors, as well as American law's general commitment to freedom even for hateful messages.

In a university setting, where intellectual freedom is especially important, there are similar concerns that campus officials, such as university presidents, not convert their "bully pulpit" into a pulpit for bullying speakers whose views they oppose. A university should avoid creating even the appearance of ideological orthodoxy. As the Supreme Court declared in an often-quoted line: "[A]cademic freedom is of transcendent value to all of us, and not merely to the teachers concerned. [T]he First Amendment . . . does not tolerate laws that cast a pall of orthodoxy over the classroom."

The importance of this ideological neutrality was well stated by the 1967 Kalven Report, whose chief author was University of Chicago law professor Harry Kalven, a preeminent First Amendment scholar and advocate. In order to fulfill its unique mission of "sustain[ing] an extraordinary environment of freedom of inquiry" and encouraging "the widest diversity of views within its own community," the report states, a university should embrace "a heavy presumption against . . . expressing opinions on the political and social issues of the day."

In light of the foregoing academic freedom concerns, one might argue that university officials, acting in their official capacities, should refrain from engaging in *any* responsive counterspeech, even in response to speech that is clearly hateful. University of Chicago law professor Geoffrey Stone—who, like Kalven, is a leading First Amendment scholar and advocate—supports this stance, arguing that "[w]henever a university arrogates to itself the authority to 'declare' certain positions to be 'true' or 'false,' it necessarily chills the freedom of its faculty and students to take contrary—officially disapproved—positions."

Let me suggest a plausible alternative strategy that both honors academic freedom and enables the university to stake out its own positions on fundamental issues: a university should be able to engage in proactive counterspeech by issuing an affirmative statement of general principles that it champions, which should include not only freedom of speech and academic freedom, but also equality, diversity, and inclusivity. Such a broad, forward-looking statement should also explain that university officials' "no comment" policy toward specific controversial expression by members of the campus community should not be construed as endorsing any such expression, but rather as reflecting the university's fidelity to academic freedom.

If university officials choose to engage in institutional counterspeech, specifically criticizing particular hateful or other disfavored messages, then they should also emphasize their support for the freedom of all members of the university community to express contrary views, to minimize the risk that the officials' statements will chill discussion and dissent. A good model for this approach was a letter that Harvard University president Derek Bok circulated to the Harvard community in 1984 in response to a sexist flyer that an undergraduate fraternity had distributed. Bok's letter explained why the students who had written the flyer should not be subjected to any official discipline, consistent with free speech principles, but it then denounced the flyer's ideas and explained why this denunciation did not abridge the free speech rights of the flyer's authors, as follows:

> The wording of the [flyer] was so extreme and derogatory to women that I wanted to communicate my disapproval publicly, if only to make sure that no one could gain the false impression that the Harvard administration harbored any sympathy or complacency toward . . . the letter. Such action does not infringe on free speech. Indeed, statements of disagreement are part and parcel of the open debate that freedom of speech is meant to encourage; the right to condemn a point of view is as protected as the right to express it. Of course, I recognize that even verbal disapproval by persons in positions of authority may have inhibiting effects on students. Nevertheless, this possibility is not sufficient to outweigh the need for officials to speak out on matters of significance to the community—provided, of course, that they take no action to penalize the speech of others.

Outreach and Interaction

> "Making progress on civil rights depends on each of [us]. Even small actions . . . can make a difference."
> —Vernon E. Jordan, Jr., civil rights activist

Government and private-sector institutions should reach out to traditionally underrepresented groups in order to promote desegregation, diversity, and interaction among all societal groups. In our private lives as well, we should strive to get to know, and to work and interact with, members of all societal groups, especially those particularly subject to discrimination. This will enrich our lives, and also help to reduce discrimination and division in society.

Social science studies have confirmed what everyday experience suggests: that the most effective way to decrease people's negative attitudes toward members of any societal group is to give them an opportunity to get to know one another. As noted above, the "intergroup contact theory" was first formulated by Harvard professor Gordon Allport in his trailblazing 1954 book *The Nature of Prejudice*. Allport posited that interaction is especially constructive in settings such as school, work, and community groups, where people collaborate on common endeavors. Allport's findings have been corroborated by a vast social science literature documenting that intergroup contact plays a vital role in reducing prejudice and promoting a more tolerant, integrated, and harmonious society. The evidence demonstrates that contact overcomes prejudice and forges positive relationships among people from many different groups, including racial and ethnic groups, the elderly, LGBT persons, mentally ill people, persons with disabilities, and AIDS victims. A 1993 study of heterosexuals' attitudes toward gay men, for example, found that the extent of contact predicted these attitudes better than any other variable, including political ideology, and a 2001 meta-analysis of 500 studies about contact theory concluded that greater understanding between groups can be facilitated by essentially any contact.

More Inclusive Campuses

Much of the recent ferment about racial injustice and inadequate inclusiveness of traditionally marginalized groups has occurred on college campuses. Most students who are working with Black Lives Matter and similar organizations to remedy these problems advocate a range of corrective measures, not including "hate speech" laws. This point was stressed by Shaun Harper, executive director of the Center for the Study of Race and Equity in Education at the University of Pennsylvania. His center has conducted dozens of investigations of the racial climate on campuses across the country, and he reported that when he and his center colleagues ask "students of color . . . what corrective actions they want administrators to take on their campuses, they say nothing about . . . speech codes":

> They tell us they want to be heard, understood and taken seriously. They want white people to recognize the harmful effects of their words and actions. They want greater inclusion of culturally diverse perspectives in the curriculum, more resources for ethnic studies programs and cultural centers, more people of color in professorships and senior administrative roles. They want educators on their campuses to be more highly skilled at teaching diverse student populations and fostering inclusive learning environments where every student feels respected. They want names of slave owners removed from buildings and statues of white supremacists taken down.

Social science studies have confirmed the efficacy of these non-censorial measures in reducing prejudice and societal disharmony. As discussed above, a massive literature has demonstrated that intergroup contact thwarts prejudice, and its positive potential may be greatest when people collaborate on mutual endeavors, which is especially feasible on campus. Additional studies have shown that learning more about other groups' cultures also promotes more positive attitudes toward members of those groups.

Self-Restraint

> "In Europe, we have more legal limitations on speech but less social pressure, while in the U.S. you have very few legal limits but far more social pressure."
>
> —Flemming Rose, Danish journalist

Just because one has the right to say something does not mean that it is right to do so. So when critics tell us that some things we say are unnecessarily hurtful or insensitive, even unintentionally, we should rephrase our message whenever we can do so without undermining its substance or viewpoint. When we choose to do that, we are exercising our free speech rights—thoughtfully.

As readers may have noticed, I have chosen to use the term "the N-word" throughout this book even to substitute for the actual word when it was used by others I am quoting, and even when they used it for legitimate, non-hateful purposes (*e.g.*, a Supreme Court decision quoting a KKK leader, in reviewing his criminal conviction that was based in part on that expression). I chose to do so because of situations I have observed where even such a use of the word in a written or oral presentation has provoked negative reactions from some readers or audience members, thus unnecessarily upsetting them, and also distracting from the discussion at issue. In contrast, I made the judgment call not to edit this book's quotation of then-President Barack Obama's forthright use of the full term to make a particular point to which that term is directly pertinent. I made that judgment in light of Obama's unique stature and credibility, including as both a foremost civil rights champion and a frequent target of that despicable word himself. These wording choices constitute considered exercises of my free speech rights in a way that, I believe, reinforces the points I am making in this book, far from undermining them. I am confident that others might well make different judgment calls, but I hope they would acknowledge that all such determinations are consistent with the exercise of our respective free speech rights.

In addition to voluntarily chosen sensitive and respectful language, another type of voluntary self-restraint involves "trigger warnings," alerting an audience that one is going to use language or discuss a topic that might upset some audience members. Such warnings should not be mandated by government or by university officials. As the Supreme Court has long recognized, forcing people to say something they do not choose to say violates the principles of free speech and academic freedom as fully as forcing people *not* to say something they want to say. But if a teacher or other speaker chooses to issue such a warning, that is an exercise of free speech. Moreover, if it is offered with the intent and effect of facilitating certain audience members' engagement with the subject, it could foster free speech, rather than suppressing it.

In addition to individual self-restraint, public- and private-sector entities may discourage the use of "hate speech," and as Chapter 3 explained, in some contexts may even penalize such speech. Many organizations have restricted "hate speech" as a matter of business practice and professional ethics. Such self-regulation is one of the non-censorial alternatives to "hate speech" laws that ECRI has endorsed. Indeed, ECRI concluded that it "can be the most appropriate and most effective approach to tackling hate speech."

* * *

The evidence discussed in this chapter supports the conclusion of many experts, including ECRI, that counterspeech and other non-censorial alternatives are "much more likely" than "hate speech" laws "to prove effective" in limiting "hate speech" and its possible harmful effects. This is the final factor in the balancing analysis that Chapter 1 summarized and that subsequent chapters have laid out in detail. That analysis yields several independent reasons for rejecting "hate speech" laws, even beyond the problems with the two assumptions that underlie such laws: that constitutionally protected "hate speech" significantly contributes to the feared harms, and that "hate speech" laws materially reduce those harms. Even if constitutionally protected "hate speech" did notably contribute to the feared harms, and even if "hate speech" laws would meaningfully help to reduce them, we still should reject such laws because non-censorial measures can effectively counter the feared harms, and because "hate speech" laws would deeply damage freedom of speech, democracy, equality, and societal harmony.

CHAPTER NINE

Conclusion
Looking Back—and Forward

WHAT HAVE WE learned from looking back upon actual experience with—and without—"hate speech" laws, and what guidance does this provide for moving forward? In writing this book, I have gained information and insights that have enriched my understanding of these issues, and I hope this is true for readers, as well.

Having been thinking, reading, speaking, and writing about "hate speech" since 1977, when the Skokie controversy erupted, I had reached a point many years ago when I refused to accept any more invitations to do any additional writing on this issue. I believed that I had nothing new to say, and that all arguments on all sides of the topic had been thoroughly aired in the voluminous writings on the subject, most of which had been authored by law professors, focusing primarily on legal issues about free speech and equality. Although I remained passionately committed to my/the ACLU's longstanding view that "hate speech" laws would be as inimical to equality as to free speech, I thought I had fully explained that position to the best of my ability in previous publications.

That view began to change several years ago, though, as we started to see increasing activism on campus and beyond in support of various equal rights causes. Having been a student activist for various egalitarian causes from what was then called "junior high school" through law school, I have been thrilled by the recent resurgence of student engagement. I have been disheartened, however, by the fact that too many students and others have called for censoring speakers who don't share their views, apparently believing that freedom of speech would undermine the social justice causes they champion. Anecdotal reports, as well as polling data, forced me to recognize that neither I nor others who advocate robust freedom of speech, as well as equal rights, had sufficiently explained our position. We clearly had not persuaded many students and others that equal justice for all depends on full freedom of speech for all. Therefore, I welcomed the challenge of writing this book in the hope of supporting that conclusion more clearly and persuasively than I and others had done before.

The process of researching and writing this book has been eye-opening for me. I realized not only that I could make my past arguments more cogently than I previously had done, but also that I could go beyond them. Most importantly, I have drawn upon significant developments since I last wrote about this topic. The upshot is that I am more appreciative than ever of U.S. law's nuanced position in drawing the line between punishable and protected "hate speech." Moreover, I am more convinced than ever of the harms that would flow from suppressing constitutionally protected "hate speech," and of the benefits that will continue to flow from the increasingly vigorous, sophisticated counterspeech and other non-censorial countermeasures that government officials, civil society groups, and individual community members have been actively pursuing. I am especially encouraged by the energetic speech and activism by people who are subject to hateful, discriminatory speech and conduct. Far from being silenced, they are being roused to raise their voices.

A disproportionate amount of the writing about "hate speech," starting with the explosion of interest in this topic in the 1980s, has been authored by lawyers. More recently, we have seen more diverse scholarship about the subject of "hate" by a range of social scientists. In 1992, the interdisciplinary Institute of Hate Studies was founded at Gonzaga University, which simultaneously launched the interdisciplinary *Journal of Hate Studies*. Similar programs have been instituted on other campuses, and colleges and universities have been adding interdisciplinary courses about hate to their curricula. Discussions about the topic also have been flourishing in the general public media.

As a lawyer, it is somewhat humbling to peruse these recently proliferating materials, because relatively few of them address the legal issues that have dominated lawyers' prolific writings on the subject. This reminds me of Mark Twain's famous aphorism: "If the only tool you have is a hammer, then every problem looks like a nail." Understandably, the groundbreaking law professors who addressed this issue decades ago suggested legal tools—most notably, new laws—for addressing the potential harm they feared constitutionally protected "hate speech" might cause. Since then, though, many diverse experts, with more diverse toolkits, have been developing alternative—and more effective—strategies.

I note the positive steps of the past few decades not to suggest that we should rest on our laurels, content with the progress we have made, but rather for the opposite reason: to shore up our resolve to continue fighting for all the important goals at stake: liberty, equality, and democracy, as well as individual well-being and societal harmony. The progress we already have made—through more speech, not less—should encourage us to stay the course. *All of us must exercise what is the most essential right of all, for promoting these vital causes: the right not to remain silent.*

Index

...

Australia, 28, 139, 148–149, 174
Austria, 29, 99, 112
Azadliq (newspaper), 85
Azerbaijan, 85

Bad tendency test, xx-xi, 7, 13, 40, 45, 111,
  123, 158
Baker, C. Edwin, 171
Baker, Dennis J., 131
Bardot, Brigitte, 29
Bazrafkan, Firoozeh, 98
Beauharnais v. Illinois (1952), 44–46
Belgium, 103
Benesch, Susan, 32
Benghazi, attack on U.S. Embassy in
  (2012), 175
Beyoncé, 55
Bias crimes, xxi, 66
Bible, 27, 28–29, 80, 128
Bierre, Pierre, 150
Black Liberation Movement (UK), 87
Black Lives Matter (BLM) movement, 11,
  17, 55, 58, 93, 132, 178
Black Looks: Race and Representation
  (hooks), 87
Black Power, 55
Blasphemy. *See* Religion
Bok, Derek, 18, 176
Boomerang effect, 146
Borovoy, Alan, 88, 135
Bowal, Peter, 147
Brandeis, Louis, 7, 38, 40–41, 75, 158
Brandenburg v. Ohio (1969), 62
Brennan, William, 38
Britain
  "hate speech" laws in, 25, 29, 138
  "hate speech" laws used against minority
    or political speakers in, 83, 84,
    86–87, 96–97
  "hate speech" violations in, 27, 28
  racism in, 29, 138, 149
British National Union of Students
  (NUS), 88
Brown v. Board of Education (1954), 38
Brown University, 2
Brugger, Winfried, 67
Buchenwald, 134
Butler v. The Queen (1992), 90–91
BuzzFeed News, 130

Calhoun, John C., 16
Callamard, Agnes, 83, 138

Calleros, Charles, 166–167
Calvert, Clay, 122
Campuses
  activism against discrimination on, 125,
    132, 184
  counterspeech response instead of "hate
    speech" code, 166–167, 174–177
  courses and programs offered to explore
    discrimination and "hate speech,"
    170–171, 185
  "hate speech" codes, 14, 34, 65, 72, 77,
    88–90, 113, 116, 129, 136–137, 166
  "hate speech" equated with violent
    criminal conduct, 2
  "hate speech" incidents reported
    (2016–2017), 130
  inclusiveness, need for, 2, 178–179
  interdisciplinary courses about hate, 185
  "no comment" policies of school
    administrators, 176
  in private sector, 30, 33
  SPLC guide to curb alt-right's campus
    recruitment, 161–162
  strict liability approach toward "hate
    speech," 111
  suppression of "hate speech," 6, 18–19,
    33, 88, 151
Canada
  chilling effect of "hate speech" laws
    in, 100
  expanding "hate speech" laws in, 103
  "hate speech" laws in, 29, 75–76, 78,
    87–88, 135
  ineffective attempts to enforce "hate
    speech" laws in, 146–147, 148
  pornography as form of "hate speech"
    in, 90–91
Catholic Church, 28–29
Censorship. *See also* Government regulation
  of speech; "Hate speech" laws
  alternatives to. *See* Non-censorial
    strategies
  calls to censor controversial
    speech, 20–21
  of counterspeech, 144
  driving discriminatory expression
    underground, 143–145
  equal rights causes thwarted by, 81
  Facebook's role, 32, 93–94. *See also*
    Facebook
  of "hate speech," 4–7, 13. *See also* "Hate
    speech" laws